The Justice Imperative

How Hyper-Incarceration Has
Hijacked
The American Dream

**A collaborative examination of Connecticut's
Criminal Justice and Corrections System
by The Malta Justice Initiative of Connecticut
and professionals involved in the system**

Elsa,
Thank you
coming abt
important

D1502547

Marilyn D. Kendy

THE JUSTICE IMPERATIVE

All photos and graphics by permission of their owners, subjects and/or the Connecticut Department of Correction, or are in the public domain.

Edited by Jim Zebora

DEDICATION

To all those who selflessly work in our criminal justice and corrections system for the rights of victims, the protection of the public and the rehabilitation of offenders.

CONTENTS

FOREWORD

Our criminal justice system is in need of reform. Such system costs the taxpayer too much, fails at rehabilitation, exacts a life-long toll on offenders and does not yield corresponding societal benefits. Of late, the political left and right have found common ground in advocating for change. This book is the product of a bipartisan coalition in Connecticut of businesspeople, correctional professionals, legislators, judges, law enforcement professionals, lawyers, clergy and academics. We believe there are systemic solutions capable of saving money, making us safer, and providing offenders with a pathway toward reformation and reintegration.

The purpose of this book is three-fold: (1) to provide information about the causes and extent of the problems overwhelming the process of criminal justice in Connecticut; (2) to explain why reform is long overdue and in our collective best interest; and (3) to suggest reforms that are supported by empirical evidence from other states.

The long-term political shift from being tough on crime in the 1970s and 1980s to today's call for reform is illustrated by the unusual circumstance whereby the *New York Times* and the *Wall Street Journal* each recently ran editorials in favor of similar reform measures.

The current non-partisan environment raises the prospect for reform. Such reform would not have been imaginable a decade ago. Having an electorate knowledgeable about the core issues may facilitate the political process. Motivation is found in both the budget-breaking financial costs and the human and community costs inherent in the current system.

This book does not seek to assign fault for the current shortcomings. The criminal justice system we have today reflects what society has demanded of our elected officials since the 1970s. Our current situation has its ideological roots in catch phrases such as "lock the door and throw away the key," "if you did the crime, you have to do the time," and "they got what they deserve." The Cheshire murders in 2007, in which a mother and her two daughters were assaulted and killed in their home by two recently released career criminals, reinforced such sentiments.

As a society, we have become hardened toward felons. Historically, there has been little societal support for the imprisoned or their families. It is generally considered political suicide to be perceived as soft on crime. This political paralysis has impeded efforts to be "smart on crime." With the support of responsible, informed citizens, elected officials will be more inclined to devote their attention to reforming the financially burdensome and socially destructive aspects of the present system.

It is the collective view of the Editorial Board of this book that being smart on crime can enhance public safety by redirecting resources toward rehabilitation and treatment, reducing recidivism, lowering overall operating costs, providing fairer justice and lessening the damage to our communities.

In advocating for reform, we recognize that victims' rights must not be minimized. Many offenders have committed heinous crimes. Such crimes warrant severe punishment, including the removal of offenders' status as free members of society and the curtailment of their ability to inflict further harm on the general public. We accept that the personal losses suffered by crime victims and their families are devastating and irreparable. Victims are entitled to the closure afforded through the judicial process.

At the same time, we note that over 95 percent of offenders are released back to our communities, often unsupervised and ill-equipped to succeed. Once branded a felon, an offender is subjected to the modern-day equivalent of a scarlet letter. That stigma and other obstacles block the path toward lawful behavior. The individual suffers, the community suffers, recidivism increases and the taxpayer foots the bill.

MALTA JUSTICE INITIATIVE

It is in the public's interest to have released offenders rehabilitated and motivated to be law-abiding, taxpaying members of their families and communities. By recognizing the human dignity of all offenders and enabling them to realize redemption and restore their relationships within the community, all of society is ennobled.

Our analysis examines not only the current criminal justice system and incarceration practices in Connecticut, but also the best practices in other states and countries. Such practices and empirical evidence strongly indicate that we can rightsize our prison population, bring down costs, lower recidivism and increase public safety, while affording ex-offenders greater opportunities to turn their lives around and reintegrate into mainstream society.

It is our fervent hope that by educating the public about the serious issues confronting the criminal justice system, hearts and minds will be changed, thereby enhancing the potential for more positive outcomes and needed reform.

On behalf of the Editorial Board,

William J. Fox

Director, Malta Justice Initiative

An offender at the Osborn Correctional Institution speaks with his father, a minister, who has come to visit him in prison.

currently under correctional control, either in prison or jail or on probation or parole.[xx]

This book looks at the current status of Connecticut's criminal justice and correctional systems 40 years into the war on drugs. It examines whether the policy and enforcement initiatives pursued over the course of such war remain effective or sustainable in view of their staggering monetary and human cost, including their disparate impact on particular communities and segments of Connecticut's citizenry. We also consider whether less costly, more effective and more humane alternatives exist that are worthy of consideration by the legislative and executive branches of Connecticut's state government.

On the strength of strong empirical evidence – adduced from an examination of best practices by "model" states – we have concluded that certain reforms can yield a trifecta of societal benefits, namely (1) reduced costs, (2) lower recidivism through reinvestment of the cost savings in proven rehabilitative treatments and programs, and (3) enhanced public safety.

Accordingly, we make 30 specific reform recommendations in Chapter 12. These recommendations are intended to "rightsize" Connecticut's prisons. In Chapter 12, we identify four desired outcomes:

1. **Reduce Connecticut's prison population by half within five years;**

2. **Reduce Connecticut's recidivism rate by 30 percentage points within five years;**

3. **Close half of the State's correctional facilities within five years; and**

4. **Reduce State spending on the prison system by half within five years, with two-thirds of the savings being redirected toward drug and mental health treatments,**

educational and vocational training and post-release support and supervision.

Our 30 specific recommendations are aimed at achieving the above four outcomes. Our reforms are intended to yield the trifecta of benefits -- reduced cost, lower recidivism and increased public safety. In our collective judgment, these benefits trump the case for maintaining the retributive and punitive system that the 40-year war on drugs has wrought. **Reform also comes with the potential of hitting a Superfecta, by producing a vital fourth benefit -- the Holy Grail of corrections, namely, redemption and the opportunity to create a better life for ex-offenders and their families.** Connecticut's continuing war on drugs and current criminal justice system has essentially erected a revolving prison door through which offenders pass time and time again. This door serves as a gateway for a life of crime. With each passage through the door, the odds of rehabilitation are slashed and the likelihood of repeat offenses enhanced, all at a staggering financial cost to Connecticut taxpayers and a debilitating human cost to the individuals and communities affected. The war on drugs has subjected two generations of Connecticut juvenile offenders to a system that guarantees the overwhelming majority of such offenders will spend their lives rotating into and out of prison.

We submit there is a far better approach, and the time for embracing such an approach is now. **The failure to seize this opportunity will subject a third generation of Connecticut youth to the revolving door of Connecticut's current criminal justice system and condemn many to a life of crime and poverty. There is a justice imperative that demands that we take action.**

Chapter 2: THE EXPLOSION OF CONNECTICUT'S PRISON POPULATION

Danielle Metz became pregnant at 17 and later married an abusive man. Her husband also dealt drugs. To placate him and avoid abuse, she sometimes helped pick up cocaine and collected drug payments from Western Union. After her husband beat her up, she left him and took their young kids with her. Two months later, she was indicted. The prosecutor wanted her to testify against her husband. Because she was not very knowledgeable, she was unable to trade useful information in exchange for a lower sentence. She was convicted and sentenced for life. Danielle has served more than 20 years behind bars.[xxi]

Key Questions

How has the 40-year war on drugs impacted the size of Connecticut's prison population? How does the current size of Connecticut's prison population compare on an absolute and relative basis with that of other states?

Key Observations

- <u>Myth</u>: The expansion of its correctional facilities has allowed Connecticut to get and keep violent offenders off our streets.

- <u>Reality</u>: Connecticut's prison population has skyrocketed since the 1980s for the most part by imprisoning a far greater number of non-violent offenders; moreover, over 95 percent of our prisoners, including those with a history of violence, are eventually released, often without adequate supervision.

- On a relative basis, Connecticut's prison population on a per capita basis is higher than those states which are considered models.

- Connecticut should right-size its prison population, number of prisons and corrections staff.

- A significant number of incarcerated offenders, most notably those without a history of or propensity for violence, are prime candidates for alternative punishments or diversion programs not involving incarceration.

- Other states, including New York, over the past decade have been able to reduce the size of their prison populations without sacrificing public safety.

The Current State of Affairs in Connecticut

Just as the war on drugs has produced skyrocketing mass incarceration nationally, **Connecticut has seen its own prison population soar.** In 1980, Connecticut housed approximately 3,845 prisoners.[xxii] As of January 1, 2014, that figure stood at 16,600, an increase of over 300 percent.[xxiii] Only recently has Connecticut somewhat stemmed the tide of a rising prison population.[xxiv]

The graph below shows the growth in Connecticut's prison population from 1980 through 2010.

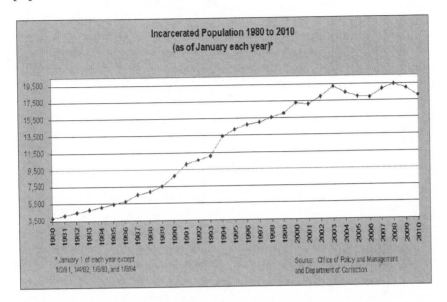

But the number of incarcerated persons is not the whole story. When one looks at the total number of people who are under the supervision of the criminal justice system (including those on probation or parole), it is an order of magnitude greater than those currently behind bars.

This point is reflected by nationwide statistics. As seen in the table below, for every person in prison, there are an additional three people under criminal justice supervision.

Population	1980	2011	% Increase
Prisons	319,000	1,504,000	371%
Probation	1,118,000	3,971,000	255%
Parole	220,000	854,000	287%
Jails	182,000	736,000	304%
Total	1,840,000	6,978,000	279%
U.S. Population	227 Million	311 Million	37%

Table: Changes in U.S. population and people under criminal justice supervision.[xxv]

Connecticut has a similar three-to-one ratio. As of May 1, 2013, Connecticut's prison population stood at 16,645. In addition to those behind bars, Connecticut had 4,139 offenders under parole supervision and another 44,997 subject to community supervision or probation.[xxvi]

So what has driven Connecticut's prison population so much higher? In 2007, Connecticut's Office of Policy and Management (OPM) and the Connecticut Statistical Analysis Center at Central Connecticut State University endeavored to identify the factors that contributed to the explosive growth from 1985 to 2005. They considered a series of possible causes, including population growth, an increase in the number of Connecticut residents reaching prime crime-committing age (18-24), an increase in the number of Connecticut residents living below the poverty line, more arrests, more arrests for drug offenses and a spike in violent crimes.[xxvii]

None of the foregoing theories proved viable. Connecticut's population increased only 11 percent from 1985 to 2005. The number of 18-24 year olds decreased 43 percent during the same period. The number of people living below the poverty line increased only 8 percent. There was a 29 percent decrease in the number of people arrested.

While there was a 46 percent decrease in violent crimes from 1985 to 2006,[xxviii] there was a 23 percent increase in those arrested for drug offenses.

The 2007 study concluded the spike in Connecticut's prison population from 1985 to 2005 was due to increased use of incarceration as the means of punishment, along with longer sentences and longer prison stays for those incarcerated. Far more people were imprisoned for a greater number of offenses and they were imprisoned for longer mandatory sentences.[xxix] Specifically, the study found the increase in Connecticut's prison population was primarily influenced by: (1) an increase in the number of people arraigned; (2) a significant increase in the number of people arraigned with charges requiring them to serve 85 percent of their prison sentence if convicted; and (3) an increase in the number of people sentenced to prison.[xxx]

It is generally accepted that most of the increase in Connecticut's prison population is due to (1) the increased prosecution of less serious and non-violent crimes, including drug offenses and technical parole violations, and (2) the corresponding imposition of longer sentences and prison terms for all crimes. See Chapters 5 and 7.

Connecticut's experience is similar to what has been seen across the United States as part of the war on drugs. The Justice Policy Institute has noted that "[v]iolent and property crime rates [in the U.S.] have fallen 47 percent and 43 percent since 1991, when the crime rate was at its highest, but arrests have fallen only 20 percent."[xxxi] Instead of making arrests for violent and property crime, police have largely focused on drug offenses, especially small amounts of drugs. Arrests for drug offenses increased 45 percent between 1993 and 2010 while arrests for violent and property crime fell 27 and 22 percent respectively.[xxxii] As the graphic below makes clear, the war on drugs has exponentially increased the incarcerated population in the U.S., even as other arrests have dropped.

NUMBER OF PEOPLE IN PRISONS AND JAILS FOR DRUG OFFENSES, 1980 AND 2011

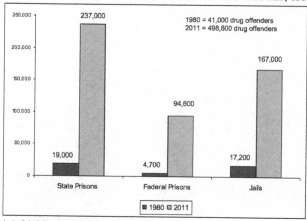

Sources: Carson, A. & Sabol, W. (2012). *Prisoners in 2011*. Washington, DC: Bureau of Justice Statistics; Mauer, M. and King, R. (2007). *A 25-Year Quagmire: The War on Drugs and its Impact on American Society*. Washington, DC: The Sentencing Project.

Best Practices

Recent Prisoner Reduction Model

A 2010 study by the Justice Research and Statistics Association looked at reforms across the United States aimed at reducing America's burgeoning corrections population. It published a set of recommendations that, if followed, were predicted to reduce prison, parole and probation populations by half within a five- to seven-year window.xxxiii Nine recommendations were advocated, the first four of which were stated to be capable of cutting state prison populations in half. Those four are: (1) reducing the length of stay for sentenced prisoners; (2) diverting technical parole violators (e.g., persons who miss appointments with their parole officers, fail drug tests or violate technical conditions of parole, as opposed to those who commit new crimes) from prison and reducing their length of stay; (3) diverting technical probation violators from prison and reducing their length of stay; and (4) diverting persons convicted of victimless crimes from prison altogether.xxxiv

The study assumed 25 percent of the current stream of drug and public disorder prisoners could be diverted to probation in lieu of prison. The study also assumed the number of technical parole violations could be slashed by 80 percent and the remaining 20 percent could receive a short period of imprisonment not to exceed 90 days.[xxxv]

The five remaining recommended reforms were: (5) reducing the length of stay for persons placed on probation; (6) reducing the length of stay for persons placed on parole; (7) reducing probation revocation rates; (8) reducing parole revocation rates; and (9) making greater use of fines, restitution and community service in lieu of probation.[xxxvi]

Texas Model

Texas is among the states that have sought to right size their prison population. From 1985 to 2005, Texas saw its inmate population triple, leading to the second highest incarceration rate in the U.S.[xxxvii] This surge led to a need for more prison beds, resulting in the construction during the 1990s of 38 new state prisons.[xxxviii]

In the mid-2000s, in the face of a call for the construction of another 3 prisons at a cost of $2 billion, Texas asked itself whether there was a better, less-costly way. The answer was yes. It chose to invest $241 million in treatment programs, create specialty drug and prostitution courts and expand probation as an alternative to incarceration.[xxxix]

These cost-cutting moves did not come at a price to public safety. In fact, crime rates fell. From 2007 to 2008, Texas saw a 5 percent decline in murders, a 4.3 percent drop in robberies, and a 6.8 percent drop in rape.[xl] Moreover, the number of parolees convicted of new crimes fell 7.6 percent.[xli] The foregoing was achieved notwithstanding a growth in the state's population.

Moreover, these results have been sustained. Since September 2011, Texas has been able to close 3 state prisons.[xlii] It has quantified the daily savings brought about by utilizing probation ($3.63 per day) in lieu of incarceration in a maximum security prison ($50.04 per day).[xliii]

Texas has succeeded by being smart on crime, while it has remained tough on violent crime. At the same time, Texas has extolled the dividend its criminal justice reform has yielded from a human standpoint. Texas' new approach, in the words of Texas State Senator, John Whitmire, a Democrat credited with leading bi-partisan reform, reflects a philosophy that "[t]here ought to be a requirement that you release a better person than the one you received".[xliv] This sentiment has been echoed in Republican Governor Rick Perry's comment "[t]he idea that we lock people up, throw them away forever, never give them a second chance at redemption, isn't what America is about."[xlv]

Chapter 3: THE STAGGERING COSTS OF MASS INCARCERATION

In 2013, an 86-year old male prisoner -- having served 40 years for felonies committed in the 1970s that were serious but did not result in any deaths -- came before the parole board. By 2013, he was confined to a wheelchair. He suffered from a neuromuscular disorder, asthma, high blood pressure and cancer. Prison officers had vouched for him as a peacemaker and protector of vulnerable prison mates. He had a place to live outside prison. People on the outside were prepared to support and care for him upon release. Yet, he was denied parole based on a "probability" he would reoffend and his release would "undermine respect for the law." As a consequence, he remained in the medical wing of a prison in upstate New York, at a mind-numbing cost to taxpayers [estimated at up to $200,000 annually].[xlvi]

Key Questions

At what cost to the taxpayer has the 40-year war on drugs been fought? How has mass incarceration impacted Connecticut's corrections budget?

Key Observations

• <u>Myth</u>: **Every dollar we spend on corrections make us safer.**

• <u>Reality</u>: **The Connecticut taxpayer is not getting an appropriate return on his or her tax dollar, particularly when one considers the high rate of recidivism (i.e.,** released inmates returning to prison within three years of their release) and the relatively low impact and diminishing returns that hyper-incarceration has had on crime rates.

• The war on drugs has come with a huge price tag.

• Between 1980 and 1985, Connecticut spent over a billion dollars to expand its prison facilities.

• The aging of Connecticut's prison population will further drive up costs.

• Most of the prison beds added by Connecticut over the past three decades are occupied by offenders convicted of drug charges, public order infractions or technical parole violations, many of whom do not have a history of or a propensity for violence.

The Current State of Affairs in Connecticut

The war on drugs has come with a huge price tag. It has spawned not only an explosion in prison population, but it has also greatly expanded state budgets for law enforcement, prosecution and corrections. In 1987, the states collectively spent $10.6 billion of their general funds on corrections. By 2007, that figure rose to more than $44 billion, a 315 percent spike.[xlvii] By 2011, the figure climbed to $52 billion.[xlviii]

STATE EXPENDITURES ON CORRECTIONS, 1985-2010

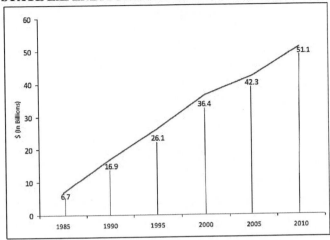

Source: National Association of State Budget Officers (1985-2010). *State Expenditure Report Series.* Washington, DC: National Association of State Budget Officers.

As the prison population in Connecticut has exploded, so have government outlays for prison construction and expansion. It is estimated that from 1980 to 1995, Connecticut spent over a billion dollars expanding its prison facilities to accommodate the surge in its prison population.[xlix] From 1980 to 2006, Connecticut increased its yearly General Fund spending on corrections from $48.3 million to $627.7 million, an astounding rise of 1,300 percent.[l] While the corrections budget is by no means the largest line item in Connecticut's budget, it has been the second fastest growing item after Medicare/Medicaid.[li] By 2013, Connecticut's annual corrections budget reached $645.3 million or 3.2 percent of the overall state budget.[lii] If one includes the added costs of the Department of Correction's (DOC) employee benefits, debt reduction and statewide administrative costs, the annual cost balloons close to $1 billion (based on fiscal year 2010 statistics).[liii] This figure does not include the costs of Connecticut's under-funded pension contributions.[liv] Roughly one in eight state employees in Connecticut works in corrections.[lv]

Forty years into the war on drugs, Connecticut has expanded the number of community correctional centers and major correctional facilities from 10 to 16.[lvi] The rapid growth in its prison population even forced Connecticut at one point to ship as many as 500 prisoners out of state, pursuant to a contract with the Commonwealth of Virginia.[lvii]

In recent years, a modest drop in prison population allowed Connecticut to shut down one of its prisons with no adverse impact on public safety.

The cost of running Connecticut's correctional and criminal justice systems is staggering.[lviii] The annual per-bed cost of confinement in Connecticut is estimated at $35,000 or roughly $100 per day.[lix] This figure rises to $50,262 if one adds in DOC employee benefits, pension contributions, debt reduction and statewide administrative costs.[lx] This figure placed Connecticut at the third highest cost per inmate among the 40 states surveyed in 2011 by The Vera Institute of Justice, trailing only New Jersey and New York.[lxi] In contrast to the $100 per day cost of incarceration, it is estimated that probation costs about $10.24 per day.[lxii]

Such costs are increasing with the greying of Connecticut's prison population. About 40 percent of the prison population is over 36 years of age, many of whom are incarcerated pursuant to lengthy mandatory minimums without an opportunity for early release.[lxiii] As inmate populations age, health care costs increase.[lxiv] For example, it has been estimated that the cost of housing and caring for prisoners 50 years of age and older in New York is as much as two to four times higher than the average cost of caring for younger inmates.[lxv]

> In contrast to the $100 per day cost of incarceration, it is estimated that probation costs about $10.24 per day.

Chapter 4: RECIDIVISM – HOW IS CONNECTICUT DOING ?

Ora Lee Hurley was imprisoned in Atlanta for failure to pay a $705 fine. She was permitted to work during the day and return to her detention center at night. She worked five days a week at a restaurant for $6.80 an hour. After taxes, she netted about $700 a month. She was charged $600 a month for room and board at the detention center. Her monthly transportation costs were $52. Her other personal expenses depleted anything she had left. Despite her full time employment, she could not repay the fine for which she was serving time and remained incarcerated.[lxvi]

Key Questions

Do Connecticut prisoners toe the line after their release or do they get into trouble? Do they eventually return to jail? What is Connecticut's rate of recidivism or reincarceration following release? How does it compare with other states? Are those states with lower rates doing things differently? Do post-release policies in Connecticut impose undue obstacles on the successful reentry of offenders into society?

Key Observations

• <u>Myth</u>: **The prison experience scares offenders straight and serves as an effective deterrent to future criminal behavior.**

- <u>Reality</u>: Well over half of releasees from Connecticut's prisons are rearrested within two years and almost half of releasees end up back in prison within two years.

- Connecticut is somewhat behind the national average and well behind model states in reducing recidivism.

- As evidenced by what other states are doing, Connecticut could be doing far more to reduce recidivism, both during offenders' time spent in prison and immediately following their release.

- If Connecticut reduced the number of people in its prisons, the significant cost savings therefrom could be re-invested in treatment and support programs that can drive down recidivism. Connecticut was one of the first states to pilot "justice reinvestment" programs. It should continue to aggressively pursue that strategy.

- Studies suggest that the first 90 days following release are critical; providing housing and a support network to releasees upon reentry is essential.

- The key long-term factor is job placement. Educational and vocational training while in prison and placement assistance upon release should be a focus of the system.

- Connecticut needs to consider measures to mitigate the current obstacles that impede employment opportunities for qualified ex-offenders.

- Connecticut should place greater emphasis on proven, evidence-based treatments and programs.

The Current State of Affairs in Connecticut

Notwithstanding the imposition of longer mandatory sentences, well over 95 percent of offenders eventually leave prison. This includes potentially dangerous people. If released at the end of their sentence, releasees for the most part are set free without supervision.

Until recently, the rate of recidivism in Connecticut had not been systematically tracked. Nevertheless, we now have some periodic data. A study conducted in 2001 examined recidivism over a three-year period starting in 1997. It found the rate for felons was nearly 70 percent (based on re-arrests within three years), well above the national average.[lxvii]

The 2001 report made an important observation: "[a]lthough the number of new crimes committed by the inmate and probation cohort groups was high, overall the crimes were non-violent and consisted of less serious property and drug offenses and crimes such as disorderly conduct and motor vehicle infractions."[lxviii]

> ...if Connecticut were to reduce its recidivism rate by 10 percent, Connecticut could save as much as $20 million annually.

The report went on to suggest that less-costly alternatives to re-incarceration for such non-violent repeat offenses -- such as "community-based supervision agencies and rehabilitation and service programs" -- ought to be considered.[lxix] At the same time, the report noted that political support and monies were lacking to fund such alternatives.[lxx]

Over the past decade, the State of Connecticut has made an effort to stem the rising tide of incarceration and devote more attention to recidivism. As a consequence, the rate of recidivism has improved, but not by much, according to the 2011 Annual Recidivism Report issued by the Connecticut Office of Policy and Management (OPM): Of offenders released or discharged in 2008, 56 percent were rearrested within 2 years; 47 percent returned to prison; 39 percent were convicted on new charges; and 27 percent began a new prison sentence.[lxxi] This places Connecticut behind the national recidivism rate of 43.3 percent and well behind those states that are considered models."[lxxii] The Pew Center on the States estimates that if Connecticut were to reduce its recidivism rate by 10 percent, Connecticut could save as much as $20 million annually.[lxxiii]

The foregoing statistics for those prisoners released in 2008 represented an improvement as compared with prisoners released in 2005: The number of rearrests dropped from 59.5 percent to 56 percent; the number of returns to prison dropped from 49.2 percent to 47.4 percent; the number of new convictions fell from 48.7 percent to 39.5 percent; and the number who began new sentences stayed about the same (27.7 percent vs. 27.0 percent).[lxxiv]

CHART 1: Two-year Recidivism Rates in Connecticut, 2008

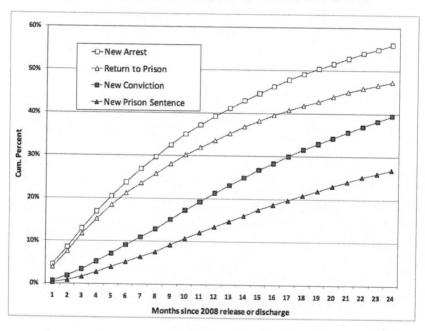

Some of OPM's findings for 2008 have potential policy and reform implications. However, comparison with the prisoners released in 2005 is complicated because of policy changes introduced in reaction to the Cheshire tragedy that occurred in July of 2007.[lxxv]

First, there was a steep drop in the number of prisoners released on parole in 2008 compared with 2005 (39 percent decline).[lxxvi] This was due to the Cheshire tragedy, in response to which Governor Rell suspended parole releases for violent offenders. New legislation in January 2008 also reduced the number of parole-eligible offenders.

Second, there was a significant decline (29 percent) in the number of parolees returned to prison for criminal violations as compared with 2005 parolees.[lxxvii]

Third, there was an increase (17 percent) in the number of 2008 parolees who were reincarcerated for technical violations.[lxxviii]

Fourth, together with the fewer prisoners released on parole in 2008, there was also a drop from 48 percent to 43 percent in the number of offenders who were released into DOC community-supervised programs in 2008 prior to completing their sentences.[lxxix]

Fifth, the post-Cheshire reforms eliminated reentry furloughs and discretionary early-release mechanisms in 2008.[lxxx]

Sixth, there was a high correlation between an offender's incarceration history (in terms of the number of sentences served) and the rate of recidivism and between an offender's age and the rate of recidivism.[lxxxi] Recidivism generally declines as an offender's age increases and increases as the number of sentences or offenses increase.[lxxxii] Thus, for example, those with the lowest recidivism rates (24 percent) were first-time prisoners over the age of 42. Of that group, a significant percentage were sentenced for DUI-related offenses. DUI-related offenses were the first, second and fourth most common offenses for older, first-time offenders.[lxxxiii] Of the prisoners released in 2005, 20 percent were over 42 years of age and more than 25 percent of those were completing their first prison sentence (780 of 2,914).[lxxxiv]

Connecticut has more recently made efforts at reducing recidivism, which have produced moderate improvement. For example, the Court Support Services Division (CSSD) (which has responsibility for probation supervision) has adopted graduated sanctions for non-criminal or technical probation violations (such as missing appointments with probation officers or failing drug tests).[lxxxv] Previously, such violations would have led to automatic probation revocation and re-incarceration. Connecticut has also recently enacted legislation that allows inmates to complete their sentences or to proceed from prison to community supervision more quickly through good or desired behavior, such as successfully participating in risk-reduction programs. However, this "earned risk reduction credit" program has encountered some political backlash. As a result, later legislation scaled the program back so it is available only to non-violent offenders and does not reduce the 85 percent minimum sentence requirement applicable to offenders guilty of crimes classified as "violent" (e.g., burglary and robbery).[lxxxvi] However, more than 30 states and the federal government have embraced practices aimed at encouraging prisoners to engage in positive or desired programming by accelerating the process by which prisoners move from prison to probation or parole.[lxxxvii]

Best Practices – Potential Smart-on-Crime Solutions

Certain states have realized meaningful improvement in lowering recidivism, including Michigan, Missouri and Oregon. All three were profiled in the 2011 Council of State Governments' report on recidivism. Oregon succeeded in reducing recidivism to 22.8 percent in 2011 (well below the national average of 43.3 percent).[lxxxviii] Michigan lowered recidivism from 50 percent to 33 percent and closed more than 20 correctional facilities from 2002 to 2010.[lxxxix] Missouri achieved a double-digit drop in recidivism between 2002 and 2011.[xc]

So what did Oregon, Michigan and Missouri do to achieve such success? Were there particular pre-or post-release practices that drove these results?

As it turns out, all three served as pilot states in the National Institute of Corrections' (NIC) Transition from Prison to Community Model project (TPC).[xci] NIC provided technical assistance to eight pilot states and suggested specific evidence-based reforms. Such reforms were premised on six strategies: the development of interdisciplinary and collaborative leadership teams; the involvement of non-correctional stakeholders, including non-profits; the provision of basic survival resources (i.e., identification documents, appropriate medications, linkages to community services); the use of newly-developed offender assessment tools; the expansion of pre-release programs; and the implementation of individualized data-driven supervision strategies.[xcii]

In examining the success achieved by Michigan, Missouri and Oregon, the Yale Criminal Justice Clinic identified eight common principles that drove the improvements: (1) collaboration between state/local governments and non-profit organizations; (2) creation of research-based evaluation tools that guide service provision; (3) emphasis on institutional "reach-in" processes that begin the reentry program well before release, including advance partnering with reentry organizations and placing prisoners in facilities in their own communities prior to formal release; (4) statewide commitment to decreasing parole revocations; (5) a combination of administrative, legislative and executive reforms; (6) the use of "short and certain" sanctions as an alternative form of punishment in lieu of long-term re-incarceration; (7) development and implementation of alternative sanctions to parole revocation; and (8) increased flexibility for parole/probation officers in determining appropriate sanctions for parole/probation violations.[xciii]

The Michigan Experience

What did Michigan do to reduce its prison population by 12 percent, drive down recidivism rates from 50 percent to 33 percent, cut spending on prisons by 12 percent and close 21 correctional facilities within a space of seven years[xciv] -- all of which occurred while rates of both serious and violent crime in Michigan fell between 2006 and 2009?[xcv]

First, Michigan created the Michigan Prison Reentry Initiative (MPRI). It did so without any new legislation. Rather, the governor's office issued executive orders to implement it and the legislature provided funding for it. MPRI was then given free rein to implement reforms.

Second, special reentry programs implemented by MPRI focused on those prisoners deemed to be at high risk of recidivism.[xcvi]

A lynchpin of the reentry program was its use of individual Transition Accountability Plans (TAPs). The TAP "specifies programs, treatments, and interventions that will enable the prisoners to succeed in returning home and reintegrating into the community."[xcvii] The TAP is a multi-phase program. The first TAP phase is initiated when an offender enters prison. Upon such entry, an assessment and classification tool known as COMPAS is utilized to measure each prisoner's rights, needs, strengths and weaknesses.[xcviii] Through its use of 130 questions, a prisoner's risk of recidivism and violence is measured.

The second TAP phase occurs approximately eight weeks prior to release. At such point the prisoner is transferred to a facility near his home community.[xcix] Another analytical tool is employed to identify both risks and needs, such as substance abuse treatment, housing, obtaining a form of identification to help with landing employment, and family re-unification.[c] During this time, service providers, specialists and case managers work with the prisoner in creating a plan for reentry.

The last phase of TAP is a period of post-release community supervision. During this period, a parole agent is assisted by service providers, including private contractors and volunteers.[ci] Michigan's Department of Corrections provides funding for such services. The goal is to provide a continuum of care that includes mentoring, the development of positive social networks and constructive community involvement.[cii]

The second key aspect of Michigan's special reentry program is the creation and funding of alternative sanctions and residential reentry centers. Such sanctions reflect a state policy of drastically reducing revocations of parole.[ciii] Reincarceration is to be avoided if at all possible. If a parolee lapses, he or she is subject to short-term intense programs aimed at getting the offender back on track, as opposed to an automatic parole revocation and re-incarceration.

Of particular note, the MPRI special reentry program was self-funded. The Michigan DOC reached a deal with the state legislature that if it saved $30 million by closing prisons, the DOC would be allowed to keep $10 million of the savings.[civ]

The Missouri Experience

Missouri was among the worst states in terms of both incarceration and recidivism rates. Its prison population rose from 19,000 in 1995 to 29,000 in 2001.[cv] Its rate of incarceration over that same period grew from 358 per 100,000 to 509.[cvi] Missouri's rate of recidivism in 2004 stood at 54 percent, the third highest in the U.S.[cvii]

Yet, Missouri subsequently succeeded within a 10-year time period in driving recidivism down to 36 percent.[cviii] So how did Missouri do it?

First, Missouri created a specialized committee by executive order, the Missouri Reentry Process (MRP). The governor also established a cabinet-level leadership group made up of top-level staff from state agencies, plus members drawn from private service providers, law enforcement officers, representatives of faith-based communities and treatment providers.[cix]

Second, Missouri identified the major factors driving high recidivism. It stemmed from an increase in the number of parole and probation violators behind bars, which was a product of an increase in parole revocations.[cx] This led to legislative reforms that allowed for early release from parole or probation of low level offenders and limitations on the re-incarceration of persons guilty of parole and probation violations, particularly technical violations.

Third, just as Michigan had done, Missouri utilized TAPs (Transitional Accountability Plans). The TAPs started upon a prisoner's entry into the prison system and included pre-release support and training.[cxi]

Fourth, Missouri made use of Transitional Housing Units (THUs). THUs are special units inside correctional facilities where prisoners are housed for the last 180 days of their incarceration. While in THUs, prisoners receive employability/life skills training, parenting training, cognitive skills training, substance abuse training, long-distance dad programs, and instructional classes on the impact of crime.[cxii] Offenders who were transitioned to the outside via THUs experienced an 8-10 percent lower rate of recidivism than those who did not utilize THUs.[cxiii]

Fifth, Missouri implemented a post-release supervision program that included swift and certain sanctions for violations.[cxiv] It also expanded the role and discretion of probation and parole officers.[cxv]

Sixth, Missouri focused on reducing both its prison population and prison budget, with a view toward reinvesting the savings in proven evidence-based practices.[cxvi] It was estimated that a reduction of its prison population of between 245-677 inmates would yield cost savings of between $7.7 and $16.6 million ($23,000 - $28,000 per bed).[cxvii]

The Oregon Experience

Oregon enjoys one of the lowest rates of recidivism in the country. In 2011, its rate stood at 22.8 percent, roughly half the national average of 43.3 percent.[cxviii] That was not always the case.

In a five-year period (2002-2007), Oregon realized an 11 percent drop in recidivism.[cxix] Since 2002, Oregon reported the largest decline in new crimes and the biggest decrease in returning to prison for technical parole violations (only 3.7 percent of ex-cons released in 2004 were returned to prison for technical violations.)cxx

What enabled Oregon to experience the largest drop in recidivism among the states studied by the Pew Center ?

While Oregon embraced some of the same strategies and techniques as those adopted in Michigan and Missouri, it also pursued a unique path. Oregon made a conscious decision to shift responsibility to the local level. Local governments (at the county level) were given far more power and responsibility for both sentencing and reentry through a series of reforms starting in 1995.cxxi This approach was premised on a belief that ex-cons are more likely to succeed if they are managed in their own communities.cxxii

As part of the foregoing approach, new legislation called for the state to handle incarceration for those sentenced to 12 months or more, while the counties took control of prisoners sentenced to less than 12 months. Counties were also charged with responsibility for sentencing conditions, parole, post-release supervision, alternative sanctions for parole, probation violations and specialized drug courts.cxxiii

Oregon also invested heavily in technology to better track offenders. It created an "offender-based data system".cxxiv One county developed an electronic sentencing-support tool that displayed for judges recidivism outcomes for similarly situated inmates.cxxv

Oregon placed great emphasis on the funding and use of proven evidence-based practices. It also established what has been described as "collaborative re-entry programs." Such programs endeavor to adopt a comprehensive re-entry approach focused on evidence-based practices, risk-assessment tools, individualized assessments and service/treatment programs both prior and subsequent to release.cxxvi Such an integrated or holistic approach focuses resources on those prisoners most likely to recidivate and provides a package of "wrap-around" services to such high-risk prisoners, including housing, substance abuse treatment, vocational training and peer-to-peer mentoring.[cxxvii] Such services are funded and provided in partnership with private service providers and non-profits.[cxxviii]

"Results-First" Initiatives

The State of Washington has been at the forefront of utilizing "results-first" assessments as a driver in selecting among various policy or program options aimed at reducing recidivism. "Results-first" refers to programs that have been subjected to rigorous analyses to gauge their effectiveness. The programs are assessed in terms of their out-of-pocket costs and long-term cost savings.

The Pew Charitable Trust and the MacArthur Foundation have worked with states, including Washington, to assess the costs and benefits of various programs. In the case of Washington, the adult programs that have undergone cost/benefit analysis have included cognitive behavioral therapy, electronic monitoring, correctional education in prison, vocational education in prison, drug courts and domestic violence treatments. In the case of juvenile programs in Washington, aggression replacement training, coordination of services, drug courts and the "scared straight" program were evaluated. Some were shown to be highly effective, some marginally effective and others ineffective.[cxxix]

Pew recently reported that six states have completed implementation of "results-first" models and presented the results to stakeholders. Three states have enacted legislation incorporating "results-first" into their policymaking process.[cxxx]

To its credit, Connecticut is currently partnering with Pew and the MacArthur Foundation to evaluate whether its correction programs are supported by "results-first" evaluations.[cxxxi]

Experience with Juvenile Courts

Connecticut in the mid-1990s enacted legislation that required juveniles to be tried and sentenced as adults in the case of serious crimes. Such laws, coupled with mandatory increased sentences and severe restrictions on parole, meant juveniles were incarcerated for prison terms of 25 years to life without parole for crimes committed as 14-17 year olds.

Studies have found higher recidivism rates among offenders transferred to criminal courts compared with those who remained in the juvenile system.[cxxxii] Connecticut more recently has initiated juvenile justice reforms, including raising the age at which non-violent juveniles may be transferred to adult court from 15 to 18. (See Chapter 11.) Nevertheless, juveniles aged 14-18 who commit serious crimes still face discretionary or mandatory transfer to adult court. This can be counter-productive as studies show juveniles who eventually serve time in adult prison tend to commit more crimes and more violent offenses upon their release.[cxxxiii] Such studies suggest a greater effort is warranted on Connecticut's part to keep juveniles in the juvenile justice system.

In addition to the recidivism benefits of keeping juveniles in juvenile court, a presumption in favor of juvenile court may also help reduce racial disproportionality in sentencing outcomes. Studies of Connecticut's process of discretionary transfers (which do not include Serious A and B felonies which mandate transfer to adult court) show that, even after accounting for the seriousness of the crime, more minority boys are transferred to adult courts than whites and the proportion of youths serving long sentences in Connecticut is disproportionately minority.[cxxxiv]

• Carmen recently moved from York Correctional Institution in Niantic to Mary Magdalene House in Bridgeport, a halfway house for ex-offenders, after serving 20 years. She is learning interview skills so she can get a job. The mother of two children in Puerto Rico would like to get involved with a dance company.

Chapter 5: THE EXPANDED LENGTH OF PRISON STAYS IN CONNECTICUT

Dicky Joe Jackson was a trucker whose 2-year old son needed a bone-marrow transplant to save his life. He raised $50,000 through community fund-raisers. But that money was not enough. To make up the difference, he began carrying methadone in his truck. He was arrested and convicted. A non-violent offender who was never a large-scale narcotics trafficker, Dicky Joe is now in the 17th year of a life sentence. He divorced his wife of 19 years to allow her to get on with her life.[cxxxv]

* * *

John Horner was a 46-year old father of three. He had been taking prescription painkillers for years after losing an eye in an accident. A friend asked to buy some leftover pills from him. John decided to sell his friend four unused bottles. The friend turned out to be a police informant who had been charged with dealing drugs. John pleaded guilty. Because of a mandatory minimum sentence, he was given 25 years in jail. He will be 72 by the time he is released. His kids will have grown up without him. Meanwhile, the informant/friend was given a reduced sentence of 18 months and is now free.[cxxxvi]

Key Questions

Are today's prisoners in Connecticut occupying beds for longer periods of time? If so, why? How much longer? For what crimes? At what cost? Are extended periods of incarceration yielding more positive results relative to public safety and recidivism rates?

Key Observations

- **Myth:** Judges can take into account special or individual circumstances in sentencing prisoners and inmates can get time off for good behavior.

- **Reality:** Because of mandatory minimum and determinate sentencing, the hands of Connecticut judges' and the parole board as well are tied when it comes to sentencing and parole.

- Mandatory minimum sentences should be limited to high-risk offenders and violent crimes based on an assessment of the particular circumstances of each incident and the individual offender's past criminal history.

- Reform is necessary in Connecticut to provide greater sentencing discretion to judges and greater discretion to those decision makers responsible for parole and probation.

- There are numerous offenses with mandatory minimums, particularly for non-violent and victimless crimes, where Connecticut would be better served by a system that places far greater emphasis on alternatives to incarceration, including fines, restitution, community service and treatment programs.

- Mandatory treatment programs for non-violent drug offenders should become standard alternatives to incarceration in Connecticut.

The Current State of Affairs in Connecticut

It is widely accepted that a by-product of the war on drugs is that prisoners are given longer sentences and are serving far longer prison terms than in the past. As part of its participation in the war on drugs, Connecticut over the years has repeatedly enacted legislation and adopted policies that have resulted in longer sentences and lengthier prison terms. Such measures have also curtailed judicial discretion in sentencing, inhibited the granting of parole and produced a higher level of parole revocations.

Connecticut is by no means alone. In 1981, many states moved away from indeterminate sentencing and embraced determinate or mandatory minimum sentencing.[cxxxvii] As an example of an indeterminate sentence, an offender might receive a 5-10 year sentence. If he or she followed the rules and did everything expected by the prison administrators, then "good time" of 10-15 days a month would likely have been subtracted from the minimum time to be served. In the best-case scenario, the offender might be eligible for release after serving 2 or 3 years of a 10-15 year sentence.

The policy shift from indeterminate sentencing toward determinate sentencing weakened the influence of judges, parole boards and, to a lesser extent, prison administrators. In many cases, it rendered irrelevant the degree of rehabilitation, good behavior or remorse shown by the offender, and it also disabled judges from taking into account coercion, abuse, addiction, or other mitigating circumstances in sentencing particular cases.

The goals of determinate sentencing -- transparency, equality, and public safety -- were laudable, even if the outcomes were not. As a 2005 legislative report puts it: "[t]ruth in sentencing was the philosophy behind many of the sentencing reforms of the 1990s. The purpose of the reforms was to restore credibility to the criminal justice system by reducing the discrepancy between the court-imposed sentence and the actual time served in prison, which had reached a low of about 10 percent of the court-imposed sentence. The reform also responded to the public's perception that 'tougher' sentences reduce crime, especially violent crime."[cxxxviii]

The experiment began in 1981, when Connecticut adopted new sentencing guidelines and abolished parole altogether.[cxxxix] Good time credits were also reduced, increasing time served by 20 percent.[cxl] In addition, new mandatory minimum sentencing laws decreased judicial discretion to set sentences and mandated longer sentences for a broad range of crimes.[cxli] At least 64 crimes now carry a mandatory minimum prison sentence of a specific duration, from a few days for DUI, to five years for selling drugs in a school zone, to 10 years for any A felony, to life without release for capital felonies.[cxlii] Of the 64 crimes that carry a mandatory minimum sentence, 15 can result in a person being punished as a persistent dangerous felony offender ("three strikes" laws).[cxliii] The penalties for these offenders are enhanced, including the doubling or tripling of their mandatory minimum sentence.[cxliv]

In 1984, the Connecticut Sentencing Commission reported that the determinate sentencing law and increased sentences had contributed to prison overcrowding.[cxlv] But the Commission found that though more people were serving more time, the percentage of serious felons in prison had not risen.[cxlvi] Most of the increase in prison population was due to sentences for less serious and non-violent crime.[cxlvii] A 2005 legislative committee report also recognized that "increase[s] in the sentence length multiplied by the thousands of offenders sent to prison result[ed] in a sizable increase in the incarcerated population."[cxlviii]

The Department of Correction coped with this prison overcrowding problem by releasing some inmates to Supervised Home Release, a new program created after traditional parole was abolished. Such program shifted authority for release from the Parole Board to Connecticut's Department of Correction.[cxlix]

The Supervised Home Release system was not successful because there were insufficient funds for adequate evaluation and supervision, and because it was used primarily to ease prison crowding. Some offenders were serving only 10 percent of their sentences. So, in 1987, the Connecticut General Assembly enacted tough mandatory sentences for crack possession as a fix to the Supervised Home Release system and as a response to growing public concern over crack-related crime.[cl] Mandatory penalties were imposed for crack offenses involving only ½ gram, while for powder cocaine offenses, at least 28 grams was required to trigger a mandatory sentence.[cli] This sentencing disparity meant that an individual caught possessing crack cocaine, as opposed to powder cocaine, was substantially more likely to serve a longer prison sentence. Crack cocaine represents a less-expensive, more available drug in Connecticut's poorer urban areas, and **longer sentences for crack contributed to racial disparities in prison populations, both in Connecticut and nationwide.** (The sentencing differential for crack cocaine was repealed in Connecticut in 2005).

During the period of 1990-1994, the flawed Supervised Home Release program was eliminated and discretionary parole was reinstated for those serving more than 2 years.[clii] The time served before eligibility was increased gradually to 50 percent of the sentence.[cliii] In addition, offenders were required to serve their entire sentence either in prison or under DOC community supervision.[cliv]

In 1995, the U.S. Congress enacted the Violent Offender Incarceration and Truth-in-Sentencing program.[clv] The program provided grants to states that reduced parole and increased incarceration sentences so that offenders guilty of crimes classified as violent offenses served at least 85 percent of their sentences behind bars.[clvi] Connecticut, which had already reinstated the opportunity for parole

> Michigan reduced its prison population by 12 percent, drove down recidivism rates from 50 percent to 33 percent, cut spending on prisons by 12 percent and closed 21 correctional facilities, all within a space of seven years. Both serious and violent crime rates fell.

after 50 percent of the sentence was served, fell in line and once again restricted parole for "violent offenses."[clvii] The 85 percent minimum applies to crimes categorized as violent offenses, such as burglary or robbery. Thus, one convicted of such a "violent" offense is subject to the 85 percent minimum, irrespective of whether there was any violence actually involved in the specific offense or in one's past history or propensity for violent behavior. In exchange for the new restrictions on parole, Connecticut received $34.5 million federal dollars for correctional programs between 1996 and 2001.[clviii]

Also in 1995, Connecticut began *requiring* the transfer to adult court of all juveniles charged with serious crimes.[clix] Children 14-17 became subject to the same mandatory sentences and no-parole rules as adults, without leaving any room for judicial discretion in individual cases.[clx]

The new prisons built in the 1990s meant prison beds were available, but alternative sanctions were not. A 2005 Connecticut legislative committee report on prison overcrowding noted that "[i]ncreased bed space meant that parole violators went back to prison instead of alternative sanctions and programs."[clxi] As of 2010, Connecticut had a parole rate (106 per 100,000) about 60 percent lower than the national average number of 267 parolees per 100,000 people.[clxii] Thus, Connecticut has embraced and adhered to stricter sentencing policies, mandatory minimums and limited parole opportunities. It has done so not only as to violent offenders, but also many non-violent offenders.

In sum, tough-on-crime reforms in Connecticut led to an increase in sentence lengths of 25 percent and diverted resources and attention away from reentry reform or treatment programs.[clxiii] As recognized by the legislative committee in 2001, "[t]he system of graduated sanctions established by state policy [was] overridden by the criminal justice system's effort to be tough by incapacitating offenders for lengthy periods of time." [clxiv] By 1984, it was known that "the percentage of inmates in prison for serious felonies remained constant, but the number (and percentage) of inmates confined for less serious, non-violent and even misdemeanor offenses increased significantly. The average sentence length for less serious felonies dramatically increased."[clxv] While tough-on-crime initiatives were intended to increase the severity of the punishment for the most serious

> As of 2010, Connecticut had a parole rate about 60 percent lower than the national average.

38

and violent offenders, in Connecticut they were "expanded to include less serious and non-violent offenders."[clxvi]

We believe that incarceration, from both a policy and implementation standpoint, should be only one of a number of alternative sanctions. It should be used primarily for those violent offenders who pose a clear risk to public safety. The public interest is not served by applying tough-on-crime policies against those who pose a low risk to public safety.

Best Practices

New York City Under Bloomberg.

During Michael Bloomberg's 12-year tenure as mayor, the number of lawbreakers incarcerated dropped 33 percent from 669 to 448 per 100,000. This reflected a 34 percent drop in the number of New York City residents in New York State prisons from 56,730 as of 2001 to 37,142 at the end of 2012, and a drop in inmates in city jails from 14,490 to 11,877 (18 percent drop). This compared with a 3 percent rise in incarceration nationally during the same time period.[clxvii] In 2012, the City's incarceration rate stood 30 percent below the national rate.[clxviii] At the same time, major felonies in New York City fell 32 percent, while murders dropped in half. The positive results were attributed to more proactive police work, innovative programs aimed at lowering recidivism and an overhaul of the Rockefeller mandatory sentencing laws covering minor drug busts.[clxix]

> In 2012, New York City's incarceration rate stood 30 percent below the national rate. At the same time, major felonies in the City fell 32 percent.

The New York State Experience.

The prison population in New York grew rapidly starting in the late 1970s and through the 1980s and 1990s. It stood at 20,000 in 1977 and peaked at 73,000 in 1999.[clxx] Thereafter, it fell from year to year and reached 60,000 in 2008.[clxxi] The violent crime rate increased in New York 3.6 times from 1965 to 1991, growing from 325 to 1164 violent crimes per 100,000 residents.[clxxii] However, by 2008 the New York violent crime rate had dropped to 398 per 100,000, as compared with 454 per 100,000 nationally.[clxxiii] With respect to property crime, the rate both in New York and nationwide doubled between 1965 and 1991.[clxxiv] Thereafter, New York's property crime rate fell by 2.6 times, as compared with a nationwide drop of 1.6 times.[clxxv]

So how did New York do it? New York was the subject of a study in 2010.[clxxvi] Researchers sought to understand how New York produced results that beat nationwide averages. Certain factors were identified. One was a reduction in the amount of prison violence. Such reduction was part of an overall plan to create a more secure atmosphere for inmates and staff.[clxxvii] Inmates who misbehaved were placed within special housing units. Researchers also cited efforts by the New York State Department of Correctional Services to develop positive treatment plans, as well as educational and rehabilitative programs for individual inmates. Upon arrival, inmates were assessed and given individualized program plans for education, vocational training and other particular needs.[clxxviii] Inmates were also given the opportunity to shorten their punishment period and earn other privileges through cooperative behavior.[clxxix] As a consequence, recidivism in New York declined. In addition, New York instituted intensive 30-day and 90-day treatment programs as alternatives to re-incarceration for parole violators.[clxxx]

Most importantly, New York made a conscious decision to right-size its correctional system by reducing its prison population and changing its composition to a larger percentage of high-security offenders.[clxxxi] To accomplish this, New York (1) embraced the concept of "merit time" that accelerated the date of release for inmates who actively participated in positive activities and (2) overhauled its harsh

Rockefeller drug laws that had imposed mandatory minimum sentencing for minor drug crimes.[clxxxii] New laws gave judges the discretion and encouragement to divert non-violent, drug-addicted individuals to treatment alternatives rather than prison.[clxxxiii]

The South Carolina Experience

South Carolina's 2010 sentencing reforms were expected to eliminate the need for 1,786 prison beds. The savings from diverting non-violent offenders from prison and reducing recidivism were projected to be $241 million.[clxxxiv]

The Nevada Experience

Nevada's sentencing reforms and expansion of "good time credits" in 2009 saved the state $38 million in operating expenses and obviated the need to spend $1.2 billion on new prison facilities.[clxxxv]

The Kentucky Experience

Kentucky's diversion of non-violent drug offenders into treatment programs rather than prison were estimated to save the state $422 million over 10 years.[clxxxvi]

• Tony celebrates his daughter's second birthday. The ex-offender who served many years has turned his life around and today he is employed as a hospital IT specialist. Tony also works as a mentor and presenter with Project Longevity, which unites community members, law enforcement and social service providers trying to end group and gang gun violence and homicides in the city of Bridgeport. He is closing soon on his first house.

Chapter 6: CRIME RATES IN CONNECTICUT – ARE WE SAFE?

Can you name the state which (1) ranks in the top 10 in the U.S. for lowest crime rates in almost every category, (2) currently enjoys crime rates at their lowest levels in 40 years, (3) has a prison population four times higher than it had 40 years ago, (4) incarcerates low-risk, non-violent offenders at rates equivalent to those for violent, high-risk career criminals, (5) imposes lengthy mandatory minimum sentences without regard for the criminal history, propensity for violence, degree of remorse or record of good behavior while behind bars of offenders, (6) employs one of every eight state workers in corrections, and (7) does so at a cost estimated to exceed over $50,000 annually per prisoner, 70 percent of which goes toward the expense of correctional officers and staff? You guessed it -- Connecticut !

Key Questions

Has our state's investment in the war on drugs and its expansion of the correctional system paid dividends in terms of increased public safety? Are we at a point of diminishing returns?

Key Observations

• **Myth**: **Tough sentencing laws have made us all safer, thereby justifying the huge price tag for hyper-incarceration.**

• **Reality**: **While we are safer 40 years into the war on drugs, most crime rates declined over 20 years ago, prior to enactment of many of the tougher sentencing laws.**

Experts attribute only 10 percent of the crime rate reduction to tougher sentencing policies.

• Maintaining the war on drugs is not worth it from both a financial cost/benefit standpoint and from the standpoint of the human toll it exacts on non-violent offenders and their families, whose welfare is best served by treatment as opposed to prolonged incarceration.

• More drastic sentencing reform is needed. Connecticut should lower or eliminate mandatory sentences for non-violent drug offenses (particularly in the case of offenders without an extensive criminal history of or propensity for violence). It should provide judges and other decision makers with far greater discretion.

• As a general proposition, the state's prisons should be primarily used to house those offenders with a past history of criminal behavior and a propensity for violence who pose the greatest risk to public safety.

• Allowing offenders, particularly those who are non-violent, to re-enter the community gradually, before their sentences expire and while they are still under the supervision of proven, data-driven programs, is predicted to be safer than releasing them upon completion of their sentences when they are no longer subject to any state supervision. Parole time ideally serves as "training wheels" for safe and successful reentry.

The Current State of Affairs in Connecticut

One might assume that having waged a 40-year war on drugs -- pursuant to which mandatory sentences were imposed, more aggressive enforcement took place and criminal justice budgets mushroomed -- Connecticut would have seen a significant reduction in crime, particularly violent crime.

From 1970 to 1990, the United States experienced an increase in crime.[clxxxvii] Homicide rates as well as other crimes were on the rise. Connecticut was no different.[clxxxviii] However, by 1991, crime rates began to fall.[clxxxix] Such rates have remained lower.[cxc] In 1969, the U.S. crime rate was 3,686 per 100,000 and the incarceration rate was 97 per 100,000. By 2010,[cxci] the crime rate stood roughly the same, 3,667 per 100,000 in population.[cxcii] However, the U.S. *incarceration* rate in 2010 was 508 per 100,000, or five times higher than in 1969.[cxciii]

The drop in the crime rate from its peak in 1991 has been attributed in part to certain war on drugs initiatives of the 1980s. Even after the crime rate began to drop in 1991, however, tougher sentencing measures were implemented throughout the 1990s and early 2000s. More punishment did not result in greater and greater reduction in crime. Nor did tougher measures necessarily result in the incarceration of the most dangerous offenders.

For example, according to a 2005 study by Connecticut's Office of Policy and Management, 80 percent of the charges involving mandatory minimums were brought primarily against drug and DUI offenders.[cxciv] Those charged under such statutes were rarely convicted of them. The study concluded that mandatory minimum statutes were not serving the function of keeping dangerous felons in prison for longer sentences. Rather, they served as plea bargain tools to process more drug and non-violent crimes through a revolving-door prison system, rather than addressing root issues of addiction, mental illness and joblessness. As one example, the study cited the imposition of harsher sentences for drug crimes within school zones. Because of the broad geographic reach of school zones (1,500 feet), mandatory school zone sentencing add-ons became commonplace plea bargain tools, particularly in urban areas such as New Haven and Hartford.

Connecticut, relatively speaking, is among the safest states in the United States. Out of the 50 states in 2007, Connecticut ranked 41st in total property crime, 41st in larceny theft, 30th in motor vehicle theft, 41st in violent crime, 25th in robbery, 44th in aggravated assaults, 45th in forcible rape, 36th in murder and manslaughter and 43rd in burglaries.[cxcv]

The crime rate in Connecticut in 2011 was about 23 percent lower than the national average.[cxcvi] Based on the 2012 Indexed Crime Rate, Connecticut has the seventh lowest rate in the U.S. (2,423 crimes per 100,000 population, compared to the national rate of 3,246 per 100,000).[cxcvii] In terms of the nine Northeastern states, Connecticut is the third safest state (behind New Jersey and New York).[cxcviii] Yet, Connecticut had the second highest incarceration rate of the nine states.

The total crime rate in Connecticut in 2007 was at its lowest in 40 years. You would have to go back to 1968 to find a lower crime rate.[cxcix]

In Connecticut, crime statistics vary widely as between urban areas and non-urban communities. Suburban areas are very stable and safe. This has been the case over a long period of time. Urban areas are a different story. Four of Connecticut's five largest cities generate approximately half of the sentenced and unsentenced inmates in the DOC system.[cc] For example, in the most recent crime statistics, Stamford (with a rate of 893 crimes per 100,000) was rated the third safest Northeastern city with a population over 100,000.[cci] By contrast, Bridgeport ranked 13th (1,867/100,000), Waterbury ranked 20th (2,196/100,000), Hartford ranked 24th (2,486/100,000) and New Haven ranked 28th (2,960/100,000).[ccii]

Given what experts regard as the diminishing returns of hyper-incarceration in terms of public safety, one can legitimately ask why we incarcerate so many people and for as long as we do, especially non-violent offenders?

Chapter 7: WHO RESIDES IN CONNECTICUT'S PRISONS?

Keesha was the daughter of heroin addicts. At age 14, she participated in a robbery that resulted in a homicide. Connecticut imprisoned her as an adult. She was sentenced to 50 years. She is now in her early 30s. While serving her time at York Correctional Institute, she earned her GED and was trained as a Certified Nurse's Assistant. She has shown remorse. Keesha has been a model prisoner. She has facilitated an in-prison Alternative to Violence Group. She became a role model and mentor for younger inmates. Her mandatory minimum sentence precludes her from release until at least 85 percent of her sentence has been served.[cciii]

Key Questions

Who resides in Connecticut's prisons? For what crimes are they doing time? Are they violent offenders? Non-violent offenders? Do they pose a high safety risk to the public? Are they drug dealers? Drug users? Male? Female? Young? Old? People of color?

Key Observations

- **Myth:** Connecticut's prisons are filled with hardcore dangerous felons with long rap sheets; those serving mandatory minimum sentences for violent crimes deserve it because they caused physical harm to innocent people.

- **Reality:** A large percentage of the increased prison population in Connecticut since the 1980s is represented by non-violent offenders with treatable substance addictions or mental health problems, who likely do not pose an undue threat to public safety. In addition, there are offenders guilty of what the system classifies as "violent" crimes, who never hurt or threatened anyone. Many inmates, particularly women prisoners, are themselves the victims of abusive crimes.

• The war on drugs in Connecticut has impacted citizens of color to a disproportionate degree.

• A greater percentage of minority inner-city residents have been imprisoned for much longer terms for non-violent drug possession over the past 30 years.

• Alternatives to incarceration for women offenders, particularly those who are low-risk and non-violent, should be aggressively pursued.

• Treatment programs for women inmates should entail holistic, trauma-informed evidence-based programs that take proper account of the multitude of needs (e.g., mental disorders, drug dependencies and post-traumatic stress) affecting the overwhelming majority of female offenders.

The Current State of Affairs in Connecticut

The table below reflects the breakdown of Connecticut's prison population as between violent criminals, murderers, property crime offenders and vehicular crime offenders between 1975 and 2010.

Table: Selected Figures from CT Law Enforcement Agency Crime Reports, 1980-2010[cciv]

Year	Population	Prisoners	Violent Crimes	Murders	Property Crimes	Vehicle Crimes
1980	3.095MM	4,308	12,902	146	169,283	21,014
1985	3.174MM	5,535	12,750	119	136,533	13,499
1990	3.287MM	8,976	18,219	168	158,866	24,027
1995	3.275MM	14,598	13,211	150	133,896	17,661
2000	3.405MM	18,398	11,380	98	99,038	13,130
2005	3.51M	18,398	10,969	112	92,183	10,680
2010	3.574MM	19,321	10,077	132	78,519	6,655

As seen in the above table, Connecticut's population has increased less than 0.5 percent per year on average since 1980. During that same time period, the number of murders has remained relatively constant, the level of violent crime has dropped somewhat and the incidence of property crime is in steep decline. The most striking aspect of the table above and the chart below is the huge increase in the number of prisoners in Connecticut, more than 300 percent rise from 1980 to 2010, while the trendlines for violent and property crimes are consistently downward.[ccv]

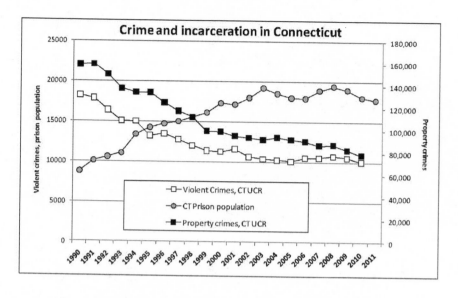

In contrast with the federal system, the State of Connecticut (as well as other states) has a larger component of offenders convicted of violent crimes. This is attributed to the purview and enforcement emphasis of state prosecutors. Across the nation, violent crimes account for 53 percent of offenders in state prisons, property crimes account for 18 percent, drug crimes 16 percent and public disorder offenses (weapons, drunk driving, court offenses, vice, moral decency, liquor law violations) constitute 10.6 percent.[ccvi]

Connecticut has a similar breakdown of violent and nonviolent offenders in its prisons with roughly half of its prisoners being incarcerated for violent offenses.[ccvii] However, because the criminal justice system supervises so many ex-offenders after release, parole violations relating to conditional releases play a disproportionately large role in the growth of incarcerations in our state. The top three most frequent offenses in Connecticut are: (1) violation of probation; (2) sale of narcotics; and (3) first degree robbery (which is classified as a violent offense).[ccviii]

Thus, a large portion of the increased prison population in Connecticut since 1980 is represented by non-violent offenders who likely do not pose an undue threat to public safety. The foregoing is likewise suggested by the risk classification system that Connecticut utilizes for all persons entering state correctional institutions. Thirty-one percent were rated 1 or 2 (namely low risk), 32.6 percent were graded as mid-level risk (score of 3), 36.4 percent were assessed a 4 (high risk) and only 102 prisoners (less than 1 percent) were rated 5 (high-level maximum security risk).ccix This classification system is used to assess entrants' risk to security in the institutional setting.

Nationally, the situation is similar. The Sentencing Project reports that "[n]early half (47 percent of people incarcerated in state prisons in 2011) were convicted of nonviolent drug, property or public order crimes."ccx Indeed, in the past 10 years or so (2000 to 2010), the Bureau of Justice Statistics reports that "almost half of the 12.5 percent increase in the estimated number of sentenced prisoners under state jurisdiction came from public order offenses, including weapons, drunk driving, court offenses, commercialized vice, morals and decency offenses, liquor law violations and other public order offenses."ccxi The number incarcerated in state prisons for these types of offenses was 72,600, which was more than a 100 percent increase in 2010 from 2000.ccxii It is estimated that over 60 percent of Connecticut's prison population has moderate to serious substance abuse issues.ccxiii

Incarceration for drug offenses is a testament to the prolonged war on drugs. From 1980 to 2011, the number of drug offenders in federal prisons increased from 4,749 to 94,600 persons, an increase of almost twenty-fold.ccxiv The increase of drug offenders in state prisons and jails was also striking. In 1980, the number of state drug offenders was 36,200.ccxv That number grew to 504,000 by 2011, a more than fifteen-fold increase.ccxvi In Colorado, the percentage of drug offenders among its prison population rose from 6 percent in 1982 to 21 percent in 2011.ccxvii Similarly, the tripling in the size of Maryland's prison system was mainly attributed to drug imprisonment and addiction.ccxviii

The war on drugs and its influence in driving increased prison population is generally regarded as disproportionately impacting citizens of color. On a national basis, whites make up 63 percent of the U.S.

population but only 33 percent of its prison population.ccxix By contrast, blacks constitute 13.2 percent of the nation's population, but fill 37 percent of prison beds.ccxx For Hispanics, the disparity is 16.9 percent vs. 22.8 percent.ccxxi

RATE OF INCARCERATION PER 100,000, BY GENDER, RACE, & ETHNICITY 2011

Source: Carson, A. & Sabol, W. (2012). *Prisoners in 2011*. Washington, DC: Bureau of Justice Statistics.

In Connecticut, the disparate impact of the war on drugs on blacks and Hispanics is overt in that blacks and Hispanics represent 24.2 percent of the state's population but over 66 percent of its prison population (mostly young and male).ccxxii In addition, despite making up only 24 percent of Connecticut's juvenile population, juveniles of color represent a majority of those admitted to juvenile detention centers and are two to three times more likely than white youths to be placed in secure facilities. Most federal drug offenders in Connecticut from 2009-2012 were black or Hispanic, male and under 36 years of age. Importantly, most of these federal offenders were convicted of non-violent offenses. For example, weapons were involved in only 10 percent of the federal drug cases in the District of Connecticut in 2012. Serious criminal histories were found in the case of only 20-35 percent of the federal drug offenders in Connecticut in 2012.ccxxiii Though disparity is also reflected in the geography of incarceration in Connecticut (see graph below),ccxxiv even when geography, poverty, and the seriousness of the crime are taken into account, racial disparity persists.ccxxv

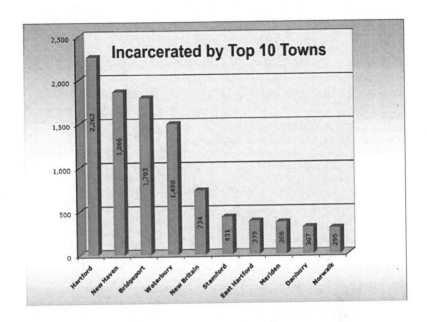

The Sentencing Project reports that on a national basis, one in every 13 black males age 30-34 was in jail or prison during 2011.ccxxvi If current trends prevail, it has been projected that one in every three black males born today can expect to serve time in prison . ccxxvii

LIFETIME LIKELIHOOD OF IMPRISONMENT

	Men 1 in 9 Overall	Women 1 in 56 Overall
Blacks	1 in 3	1 in 18
Hispanics	1 in 6	1 in 45
Whites	1 in 17	1 in 111

Source: Bonczar, T. (2003). *Prevalence of Imprisonment in the U.S. Population, 1974-2001.*Washington, DC: Bureau of Justice Statistics.

As noted earlier, Connecticut's prison population is aging, with 40 percent over 36 years of age or older and 18 percent over the age of 46.

NUMBER OF WOMEN IN FEDERAL AND STATE PRISONS, 1980-2011

Source: Carson, A. & Sabol, W. (2012). *Prisoners in 2011*. Washington, DC: Bureau of Justice Statistics.

In terms of gender, females constitute 7 percent of Connecticut's prison population and 21 percent of those on probation.ccxxviii The war on drugs has led to a dramatic increase in the number of female inmates in state prisons.

While women make up only 7 percent of the state's inmate population, the collateral consequences of locking up women are often devastating for their families, particularly those women with children. Such consequences mandate a reexamination of policies that put women behind bars for lengthy time periods for less-serious, non-violent crimes.

Alternatives to incarceration should be strongly considered for female offenders. Such alternatives should be designed to address the specific needs of women. There has been considerable research over the past 15 years on the unique needs of female prisoners. The typical female inmate in the U.S. is a women of color in her early 30s convicted of a drug or drug-related offense. She is likely to come from a family whose members are also caught up in the criminal justice system. She is apt to be a survivor of physical and sexual abuse, both as a child and as an adult. She has significant substance abuse as well as both physical and mental health issues. She has a GED, but has limited non-vocational training and a spotty work history.[ccxxix]

The foregoing portrait is borne out by an array of startling statistics: 73 percent of women in state prisons suffer from mental disorders (as compared with 12 percent of women in the general population and 55 percent of male prisoners)[ccxxx]; 80 percent of incarcerated women meet the clinical criteria for at least one lifetime psychiatric disorder[ccxxxi]; 75 percent of female prisoners with mental health problems have substance dependence or drug addictions[ccxxxii]; 34 percent of female inmates have used cocaine and 17 percent have used methamphetamines in the month prior to arrest[ccxxxiii]; 71 percent of women offenders have been exposed to domestic violence[ccxxxiv]; 68 percent have experienced past physical and/or sexual abuse; 17 percent were homeless prior to their arrest; and 47 percent had a parent who abused alcohol or drugs.[ccxxxv]

> If current trends prevail, one in every three black males born today can expect to serve time in prison.

Trauma plays a vital and often unrecognized role in the lives of women involved in the criminal justice system, principally owing to physical, sexual and emotional abuse suffered as a child.[ccxxxvi]

The three-fold combination of mental disorders, drug dependence and trauma afflicts the vast majority of female offenders. Such combination has led to a call among experts for holistic, trauma-informed, gender-responsive drug and mental health treatments.[ccxxxvii] Treating drug addiction in isolation without treating concurrent mental health issues and post-traumatic stress is doomed to fail.[ccxxxviii]

Mental illness, drug dependence and trauma are also far more prevalent in incarcerated men than they are in those men not in prison. Trauma, especially, may be under-diagnosed, as men are generally more reluctant to discuss it.

Alcohol and Drug Use Disorders: Significant Factor in Jail and Prisons

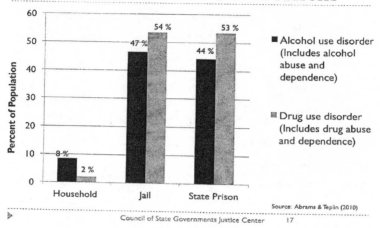

Source: Abrams & Teplin (2010)

Council of State Governments Justice Center   17

It has been estimated that two-thirds of inmates meet the criteria for substance abuse or dependence, but less than 15 percent receive treatment after incarceration.[ccxxxix] It is also estimated that 24 percent of inmates in state prisons have a recent history of mental illness, but only 34 percent receive treatment after incarceration.[ccxl]

The typical female inmate in the U.S. is a women of color in her early 30s convicted of a drug or drug-related offense. She is likely to come from a family whose members are also caught up in the criminal justice system. She is apt to be a survivor of physical and sexual abuse, both as a child and as an adult. She has significant substance abuse as well as both physical and mental health issues. She has a GED, but has limited non-vocational training and a spotty work history.

Serious Mental Illnesses (SMI): An Issue in Jails and Prisons Nationwide

Serious Mental Illnesses in General Population and Criminal Justice System

Source: General Population (Kessler et al, 1996), Jail (Steadman et al, 2009), Prison (Ditton 1999)

Council of State Governments Justice Center   16

Part of the foregoing phenomena is attributable to the current lack of, or decline in, mental health facilities. That is certainly true in Connecticut, which was recently the subject of a *60 Minutes* story, highlighting that people with mental disorders often have no place to go other than emergency rooms, which are ill-equipped to handle such patients.[ccxli] One wonders whether the lack of adequate mental health facilities in Connecticut contributed to the Sandy Hook Elementary School tragedy in Newtown.

> The prevalence of substance dependencies and/or mental disorders among our state prison population mandates that inmates be treated both while they are imprisoned and upon their release. This is particularly important given that over 95 percent of inmates will eventually be released.

Co-occurring Substance Use and Mental Disorders are Common

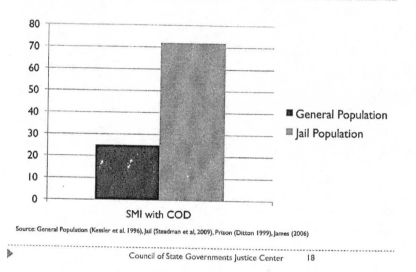

Source: General Population (Kessler et al. 1996), Jail (Steadman et al, 2009), Prison (Ditton 1999), James (2006)

Council of State Governments Justice Center   18

The prevalence of substance dependencies and/or mental disorders among our state prison population mandates that inmates be treated both while they are imprisoned and upon their release. This is particularly important given that over 95 percent of inmates will eventually be released. It is estimated that more than 700,000 inmates are released into our communities in the U.S. every year.[ccxlii]

In New York City, about 6,000 inmates with mental disorders are released every year.[ccxliii] About 40 percent of the 12,000 inmates in Rikers Island jails have a mental health diagnosis and a third of those suffer from serious mental illnesses, such as schizophrenia or bi-polar disorder.[ccxliv]

In Connecticut, the number of releasees is about 20,000 annually.[ccxlv] Of that amount, over half are released at the end of their sentence, which means they are no longer subject to DOC custody or supervision.[ccxlvi] It is reasonable to assume that a significant majority of those offenders have substance abuse and/or mental health histories that, if untreated and unsupervised, will pose a threat to themselves and the community.

• A prisoner at Osborne Correctional Institution in Somers hones his skills in the woodworking shop.

Chapter 8: INSIDE CONNECTICUT'S PRISONS – WHAT'S GOING ON?

Shenaya, 16, couldn't seem to follow prison rules. She was always angry, always getting into fights. As a result, she always ended up in administrative segregation, where she was denied programming and visits, and she was locked up 23 hours a day by herself. She would scream, yell and cry to the guards to let her out, but when they came, she would spit at them or hit them, earning her another 30 days in segregation. After spending the better part of her 16th year in solitary lockdown, she began therapy sessions and a writing class. She began to tell her own story, one full of trauma, abuse and anger – including anger at being taken from her family, first by the foster care system and later by the prison system. She learned to speak about her anger instead of just acting on it. Now she works in the library, "ticket free," meaning she is without any kind of demerits or disciplinary action against her.[ccxlvii]

Key Questions

What is going on inside Connecticut's state prisons? Are inmates getting treated for addictions and mental illness? Are prisoners getting GEDs? Are they receiving vocational and job training? Are steps being taken to lower their risk of recidivism? Are they being treated humanely? Are non-violent offenders mixed in with violent, hardcore criminals?

Key Observations

• <u>Myth</u>: **Prisoners with addictions or mental disorders who are motivated to turn their lives around can get the treatment they need.**

• **Reality:** It has been estimated that as many as three-fourths of all inmates suffer from addictions and/or mental disorders; currently, there is a shortage of available treatment services for inmates, including those anxious to get better.

• Recognizing that well over 95 percent of prisoners are eventually released (even with mandatory minimum sentences and longer prison stays), inmates who pose public safety risks upon release should receive rigorous in-prison substance abuse and/or mental health treatment and education/vocational training aimed at reducing their risk of recidivism and enhancing public safety.

• Good or desired behavior (e.g., earning a GED or completing vocational training) should be strongly encouraged and coupled with short-term incentives and long-term rewards, including early release.

• Efforts should be made to connect inmates with potential post-release support groups, social service agencies and reentry networks, particularly 90-120 days prior to their release.

The Current State of Affairs in Connecticut

Case management and service delivery in regard to reentry planning are essential components of any credible effort to assist offenders in establishing a crime-free lifestyle. One potential obstacle to program effectiveness is the culture of the correctional institution itself. Prisons, reformatories, penitentiaries and correctional institutions suffer from an identity problem. The "purpose" of a jail or prison has remained constant, but what receives emphasis changes from time to time and place to place. Prisons were initially established to ensure the containment of individuals committed to them by the court, either for pretrial detention or post-conviction punishment, but more has come to be expected.

There is little question that a prison sentence is punitive. A distinction has to be drawn which at first seems simplistic: Criminals are sent to prison, which constitutes punishment in the form of separation and a type of exile. The removal in most countries **is** the punishment. Some assume, incorrectly, that criminals are sent to prison **for** punishment, or, in other words, as the place where some form of punishment, such as penal labor, is administered. This distinction is more than semantic. It orders and puts into perspective how correctional agencies and their employees should carry out their responsibilities. Agency policies and staff interactions should aim not to punish, but to manage the prison environment as a complex social system.[ccxlviii]

In Connecticut, the punitive aspect of incarceration is evidenced by our state's continued use of solitary confinement. To its credit, Connecticut's use of solitary confinement is not as extensive as many other states. Connecticut also has written procedures governing the use of solitary.[ccxlix] Nevertheless, the United States places more of its prisoners in solitary confinement than any other country. It is estimated that 1.2 million inmates in state prisons and another 215,000 in federal prisons have experienced some form of solitary.[ccl] Piper Kerman, the author whose book inspired the hit Netflix series "Orange Is The New Black," spent 13 months in the Danbury federal prison for a decades-old drug offense.[ccli] She has worked to shed light on the pervasive use of solitary confinement in the U.S. There are reported instances of the use of solitary confinement over prolonged periods of time. For example, a male inmate in a Louisiana state prison spent 23 hours a day for 15 years in solitary confinement in an 8-foot by 10-foot cell prior to being exonerated of a rape charge due to DNA evidence.[cclii] He was allowed only 5 contact visits with family over that 15-year period.[ccliii]

Prisons serve a second function, which has less relevance to their current occupants than it does to those of us on the outside. Prisons are seen as a deterrent for those who may be tempted to commit some form of criminal act. By and large, deterrence is of some value in describing the role of the prison, but it is dependent on the certainty of being apprehended. The severity of the penalty is of less importance than the certainty of being caught.[ccliv]

A third role is ascribed to prisons. It is contained in the phrase **"correctional facility**." The term "correctional" did not enter the vernacular until the 1950s and 1960s. At that time, "corrections" began to supersede words like "penal institution," and "penitentiary."[cclv] State agencies were rebranded to "correct" crime and criminals. Facilities for youthful offenders traditionally were known as reformatories. They too were renamed as "correctional facilities." The premise was clear: prisons were given the charge to do some "correcting."

The assumption of multiple roles can be difficult, particularly when such roles are in conflict. Confinement, punishment and deterrence are complementary. "Correction," and specifically the provision of services to assist offenders, requires that institutions and the people who work in them accommodate conflicting priorities. Maintenance of order is the first priority in any correctional facility. All routine activities are structured to serve that mission. Programs and services occupy a subordinate position, even though they are regarded by institutional managers and staff as important in their own right.[cclvi]

It is easier to understand these issues in context. The three prisoners portrayed below present different challenges to the correctional system from a security, treatment and rehabilitation standpoint.

Roger Wilson was sentenced to serve four years in prison, suspended after two years, with four years of probation to follow. He is a 44-year old self-employed contractor specializing in home renovation work. He owns a modest home in Hamden. He had been a social drinker. He and his wife divorced after 10 years of marriage. As part of the divorce settlement, his wife was given the house. There were no children. Shortly after the divorce, he began using cocaine. He lined up a number of jobs and took partial advance payments "for materials and supplies." He ended up using client deposits to finance his cocaine use. One of his clients sought him out, demanding the return of his advance. Roger assaulted the client. Roger was arrested and posted bond. While out on bond, he made a cocaine buy as part of a sting operation and was subsequently re-arrested. He was re-incarcerated, did not post bond, and negotiated a plea bargain for both outstanding charges.[cclvii]

* * *

Reuben Hernandez is a 36-year old. He has been employed as a mason. One Friday afternoon, he and his co-workers decided to go out "for a couple of beers." After five hours, Reuben left the bar drunk. He got into his truck and headed home to his wife and three children. He was speeding, ran a red light, and smashed directly into a car that was turning in front of him. The operator of the other vehicle suffered serious injuries. After a long period of rehab, the victim resumed his employment at a significant loss of earnings. When he was 18, Reuben and a couple of his friends had been smoking pot together and decided, as a prank, to stage a convenience store holdup. They were all arrested. Reuben was sentenced to serve six months in jail for Threatening 2nd degree. In the intervening 18 years, Reuben found work with a family friend who had his own masonry business, became skilled, married, and was looking forward to buying a house. As a result of the current offense, Reuben was sentenced to serve three years for Assault 2nd degree with a Motor Vehicle While Intoxicated, with four years' probation. Restitution to the victim was ordered on a schedule to be worked out during the term of probation.[cclviii]

* * *

William Wilkins of New Haven fatally shot an 18-year-old in Newhallville. Wilkins, 24, was convicted of murder and carrying a pistol without a permit. The judge sentenced him to serve 60 years for murder and a consecutive 5-year term for carrying a pistol without a permit. The judge also imposed a 5-year sentence on the gun possession charge but made that concurrent. It was determined that the shooting was gang-related and was in retribution for a prior incident in which Wilkins had been shot.[cclix]

In Connecticut, offenders beginning their incarceration are the subject of an "Offender Management Plan." This is a mapping process that endeavors to set realistic goals and avail existing "in-house" programming options.cclx The guiding principle of such plans is for offenders to take advantage of the program menu and the obligation by DOC to choose interventions adaptable to the prospective length of the prison term to be served. Attainment of stated objectives may render the offender eligible for "Risk Reduction Earned Credit." Such credits can reduce the time to be served.cclxi

Staff recommendations -- based on reviews of criminal history, prior institutional history, current offense and length of time remaining --

• Cyndi, who served almost four years in a Connecticut prison, now works as an offender advocate helping ex-offenders find work.

result in an inmate's transfer to a facility consistent with his or her specialized needs and security level. Connecticut, like many other states, spends less money on "minimum security" offenders than it does on "maximum security" offenders.cclxii The term "needs" covers a wide spectrum, including, but not limited to, medical condition, possible separation from other incarcerated individuals who may be adversaries, accommodations for available programming, and the potential for disruptive behavior.

Connecticut has established a rating system for security levels which governs placement of its offender population.cclxiii It should be noted that this risk assessment is used to rate the threat that a new entrant poses to institutional order and security. It is different from the analytical tools used to assess a prisoner's needs and/or likelihood of committing further crimes upon release. The system is numerical. It ranges from "1" (the level assigned to those approved for placement in community programming) up to "5" (for high or "supermax"). At the outset, the seriousness of the offense is weighed against time remaining in the sentence. Security level designations are reviewed periodically. Such reviews can result in reduction as the length of time remaining diminishes, assuming that institutional performance meets certain standards. The long and short of it is that risk decisions are made in a systematic way to group classes of offenders in facilities that are capable of managing them in the least restrictive fashion consistent with their perceived level of jeopardy or security risk. Minimum security is less staff-intensive and, consequently, less costly.

Prisoner Wilkins, our third example, would be slated for assignment to a high security facility. Rehabilitative goals for such a long sentence would render his placement in treatment programming impractical. Nonetheless, the system recognizes the value of providing long-term offenders with constructive work and educational opportunities in a manner that allows them to make productive use of their time. In Wilkins' case, the institution to which he is assigned would likely place its highest priority on establishing management

> The United States places more of its prisoners in solitary confinement than any other country.

protocols to counteract his reported gang involvement. One of the components in the "Offender Management Plan" is the expectation that the inmate will avoid misconduct that can result in disciplinary separation (i.e., solitary confinement) from the general population. At the outset of his long period of confinement, the foregoing objective would be of prime importance. Wilkins, assuming satisfactory conduct, would remain in a level 4 facility for many years. It is beyond the realm of reasonable speculation to predict what changes can occur in correctional management, sentence reduction and parole policy over the course of the next six decades, but the DOC would continue to make available to him institutional work and educational opportunities consistent with his behavior.

Inmate Roger Wilson, on the other hand, would be slated for a level 2 facility. His offense includes elements of violence, but there does not seem to be a pattern or history of violent behavior. Other inmates in this facility would include long-term offenders who are within five years of release, many of whom have committed very serious crimes, but who have managed to establish a record of satisfactory behavior while in prison. His particular needs, assuming good health, would indicate participation in anger management and substance abuse programming. Connecticut has established re-entry programming in most of its minimum security prisons. When the time is appropriate, he would be encouraged to develop a release plan, a mandatory component of which is a Relapse Prevention Plan. Mental hygiene services would be available should he request assistance for what, in cases such as his, frequently presents as mild depression. He probably does not need assistance in financial planning, but his criminal and social history make him a good candidate for cognitive skills programming, an option that would be specified in his "Offender Management Plan.[cclxiv]

Prisoner Reuben Hernandez would also be slated for a level 2 facility, but his needs are different. He is probably subject to intense anxiety and periods of depression as a result of the problems his wife and family are facing in his absence. His eventual reintegration to life in the free community will be difficult because his role as the principal wage earner will have changed. He appears to be in the "low risk" category, but there are danger signals that would likely be identified during the initial assessment process. His prior conviction has exposed him to incarceration, and probably influenced the plea bargain leading to the length of his current sentence. He will be eligible for parole after serving 50 percent of his term, but the result of the parole hearing cannot be predicted. What would be a necessary pre-condition to a successful determination by the Parole Board would be participation in Alcoholics Anonymous. Mental health intervention would be available were he to seek it. Involvement in the standard pre-release programming should be required in order to maintain eligibility for Risk Reduction Earned Credit. He faces major challenges for future employment. Work may not be readily available upon release. He also faces a number of obstacles in restoration of his driving privileges, a necessary component for his work as a mason. DOC has a procedure in place for restoration and can assist him, but there is a mandatory waiting period after conviction for the current offense. In addition, he will be required to work out a restitution plan upon commencement of his period of probation. Participation in the cognitive skills program is also indicated. It would serve as an added tool for him in counteracting his tendency to be a follower. In the interim, he is a good candidate for work assignment at the institution on one of the maintenance crews, because he appears to be compliant, likes to keep busy and has an appropriate set of skills. If he has not yet completed high school, he can be pointed in that direction, assuming appropriate motivation.cclxv

• Audrey, who also helps ex-offenders find jobs, is employed at a Fortune 500 company after serving seven years. Today, she helps support a family of four.

Both Hernandez and Wilson are appropriate candidates for Community Release placement in a halfway house for the last six or seven months of their active terms because they would be able to obtain the assistance needed to reestablish themselves.

These three inmate profiles provide insight into what transpires from the perspective of inmate management and planning. Offenders come with varying needs and problems. Seldom is there only one issue to be corrected. Often "rehabilitation" is a misnomer. It assumes a state of full functionality to which an individual can be returned. Too frequently, they cannot. Many offenders are products of toxic environments, characterized by wanton and random violence, dysfunctional families, failing schools, dire poverty and substandard living conditions. Such environments necessarily impact what might be considered rational behavior.

The offender classification ratings influence any institution's allocation of resources between security demands and rehabilitation objectives. The designated security level of facilities determines external as well as internal procedures as they relate to staff and inmate activities. Walls and fences comprise the "perimeter," which is intended not to be breached. The extent of free movement within the facility increases as the security level decreases.

Minimum security facilities with low-risk offenders were constructed to operate as dormitories -- generally with up to 100 or so inmates in a "big box," interspersed throughout with low-walled cubicles. Headcounts are conducted at regular intervals throughout the day and night, during which all movement is curtailed. Participation in work assignments and rehabilitative programming is facilitated by the establishment of times during which movement is authorized and monitored, but not normally requiring staff escort. Dining is accommodated in large cafeteria-style dining halls. Access is handled by the movement of large groups. Minimum security facilities may have large outdoor recreation yards that can be used throughout the day. Most minimum security facilities also have gyms in which organized sports and exercise activities are conducted under staff surveillance. Visiting is conducted in large rooms at tables which allow minimal physical contact. Visits are closely supervised. There are no glass barriers. Inmates are thoroughly searched at the conclusion of the visit.

Maximum security facilities are quite different. They are generally constructed with single or double occupancy cells organized around dayrooms, which serve to connect corridors of individual cells. Headcounts are more frequent.[cclxvi] Inmates are ordinarily locked in their cells during these periods of time. Meals are typically provided in the dayrooms, under closely controlled and supervised movement. Participation in programming outside of the immediate cell corridor areas is strictly controlled and monitored. Visiting is conducted in a secure area with glass barriers and by telephone communication. No physical contact is allowed. In certain circumstances, inmates may earn the privilege of "contact visits," similar to the arrangements afforded in minimum security.

Regardless of the security level, programming time in any facility is at a premium because of the logistical challenges of effecting the mass movement of large numbers of inmates from housing areas to classrooms and activity sites, and from housing areas to meals, and the frequency of headcounts. In addition, a fair portion of time is allocated for daily cleaning, shower schedules and work assignments.

Despite the obstacles posed by the environment and the need to enforce security protocols, progress has been made to improve the provision of rehabilitative services within Connecticut's prisons.

Connecticut has done more of late relative to providing substance abuse treatment for its prison population and in focusing its efforts on reentry. In 1995, Connecticut secured Violent Offender Incarceration Program funding for several initiatives in treating substance abuse and reforming supervised release, especially for women prisoners.[cclxvii] Connecticut has also availed itself of federal grants under the Second Chance Act to fund alternative sanction and reentry programs run by non-governmental organizations (NGOs). In 2004, Connecticut also passed the Justice

> While educational services were provided to 16,905 Connecticut inmates during 2011-2012, only 574 GEDs were awarded during that time.

Reinvestment Act, which reappropriated monies that had been paid to other states to house Connecticut prisoners toward recidivism reduction efforts and graduated sanctions for probation violations.[cclxviii]

While Connecticut has recently enhanced the availability of in-prison educational and vocational training, progress has been slow and the results underwhelming. For example, while educational services were provided to 16,905 inmates during 2011-2012, only 574 GEDs were awarded during that time.[cclxix] Over that same period, vocational training was provided to 1,826 offenders, but only 390 received vocational completion certificates.[cclxx] Vocational training was provided in the areas of graphic printing, woodworking, auto repair, culinary arts and bicycle/wheelchair repair.[cclxxi] These results, in our view, are not acceptable. More than 75 percent of Connecticut's prison population lacks a high school diploma. The average inmate functions at a 5th or 6th grade level in reading, math and language arts.[cclxxii]

There is a direct correlation between earning a GED and lower recidivism.[cclxxiii] A 2013 RAND study surveying 30 years of research concluded that every dollar spent on inmate education saved $4 to $5 on re-incarceration.[cclxxiv] Accordingly, educational and vocational training must be given a high priority. More concentrated educational and vocational training with better outcomes must be mandated. Early release and other incentives should be tied not simply to participation, but rather completion of such coursework and training. The DOC needs to tell inmates that if they want an early release they must have a GED or a vocational skill. The overriding objective must be to produce inmates better qualified and equipped to succeed on the outside upon their release.

> A 2013 RAND study surveying 30 years of research concluded that every dollar spent on inmate education saved $4 to $5 on re-incarceration.

In 2010, Connecticut passed legislation reestablishing the Connecticut Sentencing Commission. On February 15, 2013, the Commission submitted its report for 2012. This report contained a number of recommendations focused principally on lowering recidivism.[cclxxv] Its recommendations covered both prison-based programs and post-release re-entry programs.

The prison-based recommendations stemmed from a white paper entitled, "Evidence-based Reentry Initiatives Devoted to Strengthening Positive Social Relationships."[cclxxvi] The thrust of the paper was its identification of a number of studies that demonstrated punitive policies are less effective than treatment-based policies in changing offenders' behaviors. It also recognized that prison may exacerbate criminal behavior in large part due to an erosion of familial, educational, community and vocational support.[cclxxvii] The prison-based recommendations of the Sentencing Commission are directly aimed at strengthening familial and community support networks while offenders are doing time. The Commission's prison-based recommendations included the following:

- **Expand opportunities for quality visitations;**

- **Promote other means for prisoners to communicate with their families;**

- **Encourage positive sound relationships through drug and mental health treatment; educational and vocational training, and religious programs;**

- **Minimize obstacles to family visits;**

- **Make transportation available to visiting family members;**

- **Make visitation areas more child-friendly;**

- **Lengthen the time of visits;**

- **Develop programs to increase the bond between inmates and their children;**

- **Revisit the imposition of restrictions on visitation and phone calls;**[cclxxviii]

- **Develop a program for fathers to improve their parenting skills; and**

- **Expand the connections between inmate and family-agency services.**[cclxxix]

The promotion of positive familial and parenting relationships is important not only in terms of the mental health of imprisoned fathers, it is vital to stemming the risk of future incarceration of fatherless children. According to the Fatherhood Coalition, fatherless teens are three times more likely to be suspended from school and 10 times more likely to become chronic juvenile offenders than those raised in homes with two parents. cclxxx Finishing high school is of critical importance from a criminal justice perspective. A 2010 Pew Trust report found that more than one in three young black men without a high school diploma are currently behind bars, and that a young black man who fails to finish high school has a better chance of being imprisoned than being employed. cclxxxi

Best Practices

The Sentencing Commission's prison-based recommendations are in line with the approach utilized in many European countries. In those countries, the focus of corrections is squarely on rehabilitation and social reintegration, as opposed to punishment, particularly with regard to non-violent offenders. cclxxxii In Germany and the Netherlands, people are incarcerated at about one-tenth the rate of incarceration in the U.S. and for far shorter prison stays (12 months or less versus the U.S. average of three years). cclxxxiii

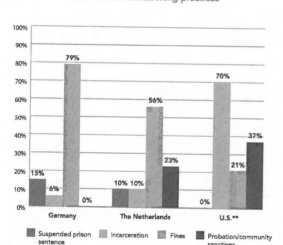

Figure 2. Comparison of German, Dutch, and American sanctioning practices*

*Year of data varies by country: Germany—2010, The Netherlands—2004, and U.S.—2004

**U.S. data does not add up to 100 percent because combinations of sentences are possible

Data source for Germany: Dünkel, 2013 ("Not Suspended Prison Sentence" included in "Incarceration" category)

Data source for the Netherlands: van Kalmthout and Hofstee-van der Meulen, 2007 ("Non-conditional Prison Sentence" included in "Incarceration" category; "Transactions" included in "Fines" category; "Task Penalties" and "Penal Measures" included in "Probation/Community Sanctions" category)

Data source for U.S.: Pettenuti and Fenster, 2011 ("Control of Freedom" included in "Probation" category; "Community Service" included in "Probation/Community Sanctions" category)

Ram Subramainian and Alison Shames. *Sentencing and Prison Practices in Germany and the Netherlands: Implications for the United States.* New York, NY: Vera Institute of Justice, 2013

The rehabilitation process in Germany and the Netherlands starts while offenders are in prison, where prisoners are given a greater level of self-control and receive considerable training. In addition, upon their release, ex-offenders do not face the punitive obstacles confronting those released in the U.S., such as employment, housing and public assistance restrictions that increase the likelihood of recidivism.[cclxxxiv]

The Garner Correctional Institution in Newtown is framed by multiple rows of razor wire.

Chapter 9: PUNISHMENT BEYOND INCARCERATION – LIFE ON THE OUTSIDE

Maurice has just completed a mandatory minimum sentence for a felony marijuana possession. He has been a model inmate. He earned his GED and successfully completed drug counseling and treatment while behind bars. He is looking forward to starting over and being reunited with his family. His wife and three young kids have had a rough time during his incarceration. Maurice had been the principal bread winner. His family was forced to move in with his wife's mother in her public housing unit. Maurice leaves prison with $3,000 in debt for court and drug treatment costs. Unbeknownst to Maurice, as a consequence of his conviction, he is now ineligible for federally-funded health and welfare benefits, food stamps, public housing and federal education assistance. His driver's license has been automatically suspended.

Upon his release, Maurice moved in with his mother-in-law. Following his release, Maurice applied for various jobs without success. Each time he was required to check a box inquiring whether he had ever been arrested or convicted of a crime. Maurice has been forced to take part-time minimum wage jobs in the fast food industry. His paychecks were subject to garnishment orders owing to his indebtedness for his court and drug treatment costs.

After six months of not being able to drive, get a job, find housing or qualify for public benefits, he again started doing drugs. Two months later, he was arrested for possession of a small amount of marijuana. He was sent back to prison as a repeat offender for violating the conditions of his parole. His mother-in-law was presented with an eviction notice because her lease is governed by the federal government's "one strike, you're out" policy. Such policy mandates the termination of a lease if the tenant or a member or *guest in his or her household engages in drug-related or criminal activity either on or off premises.*cclxxxv

Key Questions

Do we, as taxpayers, want to see prisoners succeed following their release? Is it in our collective interest for parolees, upon reentry, to stay clean, secure a job and support their families? Should we take measures aimed at enhancing their prospects for rehabilitation? Alternatively, should we punish prisoners upon their release by curtailing their access to public assistance and entitlements, even when doing so imposes enormous burdens on their families? Should we make it harder for them to mainstream into society, thereby increasing the risk of recidivism? Is the public served by stacking the deck against ex-cons and raising roadblocks along their path toward forging a viable life outside of prison walls?

Key Observations

• <u>Myth</u>: **Reducing mandatory minimum sentencing and/or liberalizing parole or early release will put the public at greater risk.**

• <u>Reality</u>: **The current system releases prisoners at the end of their sentences without adequate supervision, including those inmates with histories of violent behavior. We are better served by a system that releases prisoners earlier and subjects them to supervision and supports them with re-entry services.**

• **Connecticut should study the extent to which federal and state-imposed post-release sanctions are contributing to high recidivism rates and assess whether such sanctions make sense.**

• Efforts should be made to identify any and all reentry obstacles potentially facing offenders upon their release from Connecticut's prisons. We should ensure that state agencies and non-profits coordinate and cooperate in enabling safe community transitions.

• Specific plans of action (legislative and executive) should be crafted to minimize or eliminate each obstacle that is not warranted by a countervailing and overriding public interest (e.g., public safety concerns).

• Job placement efforts should be made while inmates are in prison.

• DOC should set a goal of doubling its GED and vocational training completion rates every two years.

• Connecticut should pursue an outreach program for in-state employers to encourage or incentivize them to give qualified ex-offenders a second chance, including tying state tax incentives or credits to hiring ex-offenders.

• Connecticut should consider subsidizing the wages of qualified ex-offenders hired by private employers during the first year after release as an incentive, just as the state's STEP-UP program currently does for unemployed residents.

The Current State of Affairs in Connecticut

"They All Come Back"

Each year in the U.S. more than 700,000 prisoners are being returned to their communities. In 2008 in Connecticut, 16,286 people returned to their communities from prison and 7,435 were released at the end of their sentences, with no state supervision or parole support.[cclxxxvi]

These ex-offenders are no more prepared to deal with the challenges on the outside after incarceration any more than they were before being imprisoned. In the 2012 Annual Report published by the Connecticut Department of Correction, we learn sobering facts about the offender population. They report about 75 percent of the prison population had experienced substance abuse problems, yet the percentage of the prison population receiving treatment for drugs is only 23 percent. In Connecticut, 75 percent of the prison population is without a HS diploma or GED -- this translates to about 12,500 persons. Yet in 2012, only 574 GEDs were awarded.[cclxxxvii] Pell grants are not available to the incarcerated. As a consequence, higher education for most is out of reach, though some universities in Connecticut have started education programs for prisoners in cooperation with correctional facilities.[cclxxxviii] A 2013 Department of Justice-funded study conducted by RAND indicates that vocational and post-GED education, even after reentry, can have a significant effect on reducing recidivism.[cclxxxix]

With all the money Connecticut is spending on corrections, one might think that the benefit to Connecticut is a group of ex-offenders ready to "go the straight and narrow."

Unfortunately, and for a variety of reasons, this is not the case. In the 2011 Recidivism Report authored by DOC, we find that more than half of all ex-offenders released from prison will be re-arrested and convicted within two years of their release. See Chapter Four. This experience is above the national norms. One Missouri study concluded that the recidivism rate could be reduced as much by 50 percent, to one out of every four ex-offenders returned to prison within two years of release, if the ex-offender were armed with a GED and a job. Unfortunately, that statistic is not part of Connecticut ex-offenders' reality. About 70 percent of offenders and ex-offenders are high school dropouts.[ccxc] It has been reported that nearly one-third of young black men in the U.S. are jobless.[ccxci] The jobless rate for young black male high school dropouts, including those behind bars, is 65 percent.[ccxcii]

In "But They All Come Back: Rethinking Prisoner Re-Entry," Jeremy Travis writes, "[t]he explosive, continuing growth of the nation's prison population is a well-known fact. Less recognized is one of the consequences of this extraordinarily high figure [of incarceration], ...This increase in the movement from the prison door to community doorstep comes at a time when the traditional mechanisms for managing reentry have been significantly weakened....Ironically, the rise in the number of prisoners has been accompanied by the loss of confidence in the institution entrusted with supervising their return – the parole board."[ccxciii]

Connecticut is no exception. The Connecticut Office of Policy and Management and Connecticut Statistical Analysis Center's 2007 recidivism study demonstrated that offenders released from prison at the end of their sentence, without any parole supervision, are more likely to be quickly rearrested than those released with parole supervision.[ccxciv]

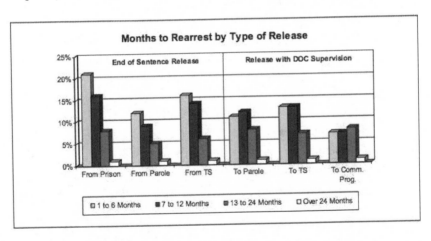

The Bureau of Judicial Statistics reported in 2002 that at least 95 percent of all state prisoners will be released at some point. They also note that about three out of four inmates leaving state prisons had been convicted of a non-violent crime.[ccxcv]

Collateral Consequences of Convictions

Michelle Alexander, author of *The New Jim Crow*, has described the collateral punishment and obstacles facing parolees as a form of "civic death" and "permanent second-class status," the practical effect of which is that an ex-offender's debt to society is never repaid.[ccxcvi]

It is estimated that 40 states require parolees to "maintain gainful employment." Failure to comply can mean re-incarceration.[ccxcvii] Yet, only 10 states prohibit employers and licensing agencies from considering arrest, and three prohibit some employers and occupational and licensing agencies from doing so.[ccxcviii] In Connecticut, New Haven has "banned the box" for city positions and the State of Connecticut has done the same for state jobs.[ccxcix] However, "banning the box" on employment applications only gets someone past the first step in the hiring process. Post-hiring background checks can often lead to the termination of ex-offenders.

In Connecticut, there remain an array of laws that inhibit the ability of ex-offenders to obtain professional licenses or secure employment in certain fields.[ccc]

In some jurisdictions, ex-offenders are billed for drug testing, drug treatments, pre-conviction fees and post-conviction fees.[ccci] Two-thirds of people in jail report annual income of less than $12,000.[cccii] In most states, probation officers can compel parolees to pay up to 35 percent of income toward fines, surcharges and restitution.[ccciii]

Post-incarceration housing is also an issue. A study found that post-release imprisonment in state prisons and city jails fell by 74 and 40 percent, respectively, when parolees were provided with supportive housing.[ccciv]

Welfare reform legislation in 1996 imposed a five-year limit on welfare benefits, ended individual entitlement to welfare and provided states with block grants.[cccv] The bill required states to permanently bar individuals with drug-related felony convictions from receiving federally-funded public assistance.[cccvi] While the legislation has an opt-out provision, only 13 states as of 2010 opted out entirely. Most states partially opted out by creating exceptions for people in drug treatment.[cccvii] The net result has been that thousands of felony drug offenders are ineligible for the federal Supplemental Nutrition Assistance Program (or SNAP, formerly called Food Stamps) for the remainder of their lives.[cccviii]

A national study found that 54 percent of incarcerated men were working prior to their incarceration and were the primary breadwinner for their families.[cccix] Following their release from prison, these men never recovered economically. The Pew Trust reports that family income generally falls 22 percent after a father is imprisoned and remains 15 percent lower following re-entry.[cccx]

Successful reentry is often impeded in Connecticut by lack of coordination between different government agencies and non-profit community services. New community reentry roundtables have been established throughout Connecticut to promote communication, so that, for example, people returning to the community have identity documents from the DMV, SNAP from the Department of Social Services, mental health and/or addiction treatment set up in the community from Department of Mental Health and Addiction Services, and housing options from community providers, before they hit the street. The first weeks on the outside are critical, because without ID, housing and basic support for food and medicine, offenders can't stay on the path to a law-abiding life.

> A study found that post-release imprisonment in state prisons and city jails fell by 74 and 40 percent, respectively, when parolees were provided with supportive housing.

Transitions are also more difficult because in Connecticut, the Court Support Services Division handles pretrial and probation supervision, while the Department of Correction handles post-incarceration re-entry supervision. Parole determinations are made by the Board of Pardons and Parole. By contrast, in the federal system, the Federal Probation Department handles all supervision of offenders in the community, whether pre- or post-trial, on probation or supervised release following prison. Coordinating the data, analysis, and policies of all of these different state agencies, and working effectively with non-profit community groups, is crucial to developing reentry strategies that make sense. This table from the Connecticut Office of Policy Management illustrates the jurisdictional complexities:

Who decides if released to community?	Types of Release	Defintion
Department of Corrections (DOC) *Supervised by DOC Parole Officers*	Transitional Supervision (TS)	Inmates with sentences of two years or less are eligible to be released on TS after serving 50% of their sentence. The DOC provides supervision and case management through its Parole and Community Services Unit for offenders on TS status.
	Halfway House (HWH)	Inmates can become eligible to live in a halfway house if they have been voted to parole or are within 18 months of their release date. Halfway houses provide offenders with structured programs and supervision to help them obtain employment, housing, education, or residential substance abuse treatment.
	Furlough	Section 35 of PA 09-07, September special session, reinstated reentry furloughs for a period of up to 45 days for any compelling reason consistent with rehabilitation.
	Transitional Placement	After a successful term in a halfway house, inmates can be transferred to an approved community placement or private residence.
Board of Pardons and Parole (BOPP) *Supervised by DOC Parole Officers*	Parole	Inmates serving sentences greater than two years may be eligible for parole. Offenders convicted of non-violent crimes can become eligible after serving 50% of their sentences and offenders convicted of violent crimes can become eligible after serving 85% of their sentences. The parollee must comply with the imposed conditions of parole; violators may be remanded to prison.
	Transfer Parole	An offender can be released to transfer parole 18 months prior to his or her voted to parole date. Offenders on transfer parole are placed under the same or, in some cases, stricter supervision conditions than offenders on parole.
	Special Parole	Special parole is a mandatory, court-imposed period of parole following the completion of a sentence. If an inmate violates special parole, he or she may be remanded to prison for the remainder of the sentence. In general, special parole is reserved for high-risk offenders.
Judicial Branch's Court Support Services Division (CSSD) / Courts *Supervised by CSSD Probation Officers*	Probation	Probation is a mandatory, court-imposed period of supervision that allows a defendant to forego incarceration. Instead, the offender is subject to specific conditions of supervision (paying a fine, doing community service, attending a drug treatment program, etc.).
	Split Sentence Probation	A mandatory, court-imposed period of supervision following DOC sentence completion. If an offender violates split sentence probation, he or she may be remanded to court.

Best Practices

"The University of Sing Sing"

After the U.S. Congress abolished Pell Grants for inmates in 1994, a privately-operated program known as Hudson Link was started in 1995 at the Sing Sing maximum security prison in Ossining, New York, to fill the gap.[cccxi] Currently, there are 334 inmates enrolled. Hudson Link has partnered with Mercy College to offer GED and college degrees. To qualify for the program, inmates must be "ticket free" for two years, meaning they cannot have had any kind of demerits or disciplinary action against them. Hudson Link also has an alumni re-entry support program to help its graduates successfully transition back to the community and reduce the risk of re-incarceration. The support includes resume writing, interview skills and job-search assistance, alumni dinners and networking events, free business suits and laptop computers, internship opportunities and links to other re-entry organizations. Most impressive is that the recidivism rate within three years of release for Hudson Link graduates is less than 2 percent over the 16-year history of the program.[cccxii]

Best Practices Identified by Connecticut's Sentencing Commission

In its 2012 Report, the Connecticut Sentencing Commission made a number of post-release re-entry program and policy recommendations based on its efforts to identify best practices. Its recommendations included the following:

- **Expand family mediation and transition services;**

- **Re-evaluate options for child care and transportation;**

- **Review mandatory public housing restrictions on ex-offenders;**

• Engage former incarcerated individuals in therapy;

• Enhance transitional housing and halfway house reentry programs;

• Provide more networking opportunities among community services providers;

• Coordinate reentry support for housing, employment and food;

• Support in-prison drug and mental health treatments with community aftercare;

• Consider options for addressing accommodation of child support obligations during incarceration;

• Re-evaluate driver license suspensions;

• Re-evaluate post-incarceration employment and licensing restrictions;

• Re-evaluate fees parolees have to pay for electronic monitoring;

• Record and track participants in existing programs for better future evaluation;

• Create a "certificate of rehabilitation" which would have the effect of a provisional pardon that would provide employers with liability protection; and provide greater guidance to licensing agencies and state employers.[cccxiii]

Chapter 10: AVOIDING INCARCERATION THROUGH "NO-ENTRY" DIVERSION PROGRAMS

Robert returned home to Hartford after serving three tours of military service in Iraq and Afghanistan. He was honorably discharged. He was awarded the Purple Heart for severe head injuries he suffered during a roadside mine explosion in which some of his comrades died. Following his return, Robert had significant difficulty adjusting to civilian life. He experienced severe depression and unpredictable episodes of explosive anger. As a military veteran, he was too ashamed to seek counseling. Robert attempted to alleviate his symptoms through the use of alcohol and drugs. He was arrested for driving erratically at a high rate of speed at 2 a.m. in the morning. A search conducted incident to the arrest found empty bottles of vodka in the back seat and a small amount of cocaine in Robert's pocket. He is concerned that his arrest and a conviction will cause him to lose his veterans' benefits.

* * *

Jocelyn is the single parent of three children under the age of 10 years. She lives in New Haven. She is a licensed health care worker. Jocelyn has no prior criminal record. She divorced her first husband after their youngest child was born. Since that time, her boyfriend, Jordan, has been living with Jocelyn and the children in her home as a fully engaged father figure. Things were going extremely well in her life. However, three months prior to the incident that would cause Jocelyn's arrest, Jordan was shot and killed in the crossfire of a gang dispute. He was an innocent bystander. Since his death, Jocelyn has battled depression and insomnia. She started smoking marijuana at night to help numb the pain of her loss and to sleep. One evening, she caused a motor vehicle accident, resulting in injuries to the driver of another car. When police searched her car, she was found to be in possession of marijuana. She was released on bond, but the prosecutor is insisting that any plea bargain must involve jail time. Jocelyn will lose both her stable housing and employment. She is worried that if she is incarcerated, her children will be placed in custody of the Department of Children and Families, causing them further emotional trauma after Jordan's recent death.

* * *

Eduardo is a 49-year-old citizen of Guatemalan living in Hartford. He has a green card. He and his family, including his children, have been living in the U.S. for 15 years. His children were born in the United States and therefore are U.S. citizens. Eduardo is arrested for public intoxication, providing liquor to a minor and breach of peace. He is referred to the Hartford Community Court docket. He is told that if he enters a guilty plea and completes the community service as required by the court, his guilty plea will then be vacated in 30 days and he will not have a record. He is concerned that this court process will cause him to be deported to Guatemala without his family.

Key Questions

Are there options in Connecticut by which these three individuals can avoid incarceration?[cccxiv] Can they be diverted from serving jail time and placed in an alternative program? Do such programs strike the right balance among punishment, retribution, deterrence, rehabilitation and victim compensation? Do all diversion programs dismiss and/or erase the charges if the defendant successfully completes the program? How are diversion programs evaluated for effectiveness? Are diversion programs equally available regardless of race, ethnicity, gender, immigration status and language barriers? How long is the average waiting period to access a pretrial diversion program for incarcerated individuals? Are diversion programs granted early enough in the pretrial process to avoid the negative impact and collateral consequences of arrest and incarceration?

Key Observations

• <u>Myth</u>: Everyone in prison deserves to be there and pay their debt to society.

• <u>Reality</u>: Not all offenders warrant time in prison. Their particular offenses, criminal history, individual circumstances and needs may suggest that their interests and those of the public are better served by placing them in a diversion treatment program as an alternative to incarceration, and at a lower cost to taxpayers.

• Diversion programs that carry with them the potential for expunging arrests or convictions from an offender's record can serve as a great motivation for offenders to complete treatment and stay clean.

• Greater coordination is warranted among the different state agencies and courts responsible for pretrial supervision and admission to diversion programs.

• Connecticut should develop an accurate and detailed offender database and procure software analytical tools that track, evaluate and analyze, both on an aggregated and individualized basis, convictions, criminal histories, sentences, jail stays, prison stays, probation and parole histories, diversion programs, rehabilitation and recidivism. Such database and analytical tools must be accessible by all agencies and stakeholders in the system, including judges, DOC, CSSD, the Board of Parole, parole officers, probation officers, the Sentencing Commission and OPM.

• Connecticut should review and explore ways to mitigate the stigma, obstacles and collateral consequences faced by offenders who successfully complete diversion programs and stay clean.

The Current State of Affairs in Connecticut

For the past two decades, Connecticut has been on the forefront of developing programs to divert defendants from the criminal justice system without a criminal record and/or without incarceration.[cccxv] Generally a diversion program allows persons charged with crimes to avoid prosecution and incarceration by successfully completing court-sanctioned, community-based treatment programs or conditions.[cccxvi] Without them, many persons charged with crimes would never receive the mental health or substance abuse treatment they need to improve their lives. They would also have a criminal record that would present considerable barriers to living a more productive life.[cccxvii] But in order to be truly effective, court diversionary programs must be provided quickly to arrested persons who are eligible and unable to make bond.[cccxviii] Although some diversion programs may be granted at arraignment, others may not be granted to a defendant until days, weeks or months of incarceration have been served,[cccxix]

The opportunities for diversion from the criminal justice system occur at many points throughout the process from pre-arrest to sentencing after conviction. In the most immediate situations, it is the decision by the police whether to arrest or not arrest a person for their conduct. Some police departments provide crisis intervention training for their officers to recognize and divert mentally ill individuals to hospitals rather than subjecting them to arrest and possible incarceration.

If arrest occurs, defendants may represent themselves (pro-se), hire private counsel or, if indigent, obtain the services of a public defender to assist them at their first court appearance. At that first appearance, if enough information is brought to the attention of the court and prosecutor, defendants may be able to apply for diversionary programs if they meet eligibility requirements. For example, a defendant charged with first offense DUI or another criminal offense may apply for diversion at that first appearance through the alcohol education program (AEP) or Accelerated Rehabilitation (AR), if he/she meets eligibility requirements. Defendants exhibiting significant mental health histories may be diverted immediately from court with conditions ordered for treatment.

Alternatively, the defendant may request a continuance to meet certain conditions to settle the case. For example, if the defendant has no record, the prosecutor may agree to continue the case for the individual to bring in proof that they performed community service, obtained counseling, or made financial restitution to a victim, in exchange for dismissing or entering a nolle on the charges.

If the defendant is not eligible for diversion at arraignment due to lack of relevant information about the facts of the case or the defendant's record, and the defendant is incarcerated for failure to make bond, defense counsel may request referral of the case to the Court Support Services Jail Re-interview Program (CSSD JRI). JRI personnel will re-interview the defendant in the correctional facility to determine whether the individual is eligible for a diversionary program. If so, JRI staff and defense counsel will notify the court of the client's eligibility for diversion at the next court appearance. Diversionary program options may also be discussed at subsequent pretrial conferences between defense counsel and the prosecutor.

> A diversion program allows persons charged with crimes to avoid prosecution and incarceration by successfully completing court-sanctioned, community-based treatment programs or conditions.

If the defendant is convicted of a crime, either by a guilty plea or trial, defense counsel may also present an alternative to incarceration sentencing plan to the court if the prosecutor is requesting a prison sentence. These comprehensive plans offer the court options to hold the defendant accountable in the community in lieu of prison, while ensuring the safety of the community.

Despite the numerous diversion initiatives offered by the Connecticut criminal justice system, many defendants and their families are still economically and emotionally devastated due to

the collateral consequences of arrest and pretrial incarceration.[cccxx]
**This is true even when the case is resolved without a sentence of
incarceration or conviction. For example, in each of the three
defendant scenarios above, the mere fact of an arrest and pretrial
incarceration or even participation in a diversion program that
requires admission of wrongdoing can cause the loss of
employment, permits and licensure for certain jobs**[cccxxi]**, public
benefits,**[cccxxii] **subsidized housing**[cccxxiii]**, military benefits**[cccxxiv]**, denial of
student loans**[cccxxv]**, termination of parental rights**[cccxxvi] **and
deportation.**[cccxxvii]

Incarcerated individuals, especially those who are indigent or the
working poor, may lose employment, stable housing, personal
possessions, and established community ties very quickly. Being granted
a diversionary program may not avoid such losses and may exacerbate
the situation.[cccxxviii] Diversionary programs may require substantial entry
and participation fees even if the defendant is indigent, which may
preclude participation if the fees are not waived by the court or the
program.[cccxxix]

There is currently insufficient capacity in community and
residential treatment programs to divert many incarcerated pretrial
defendants in a timely fashion. Many defendants spend long periods of
time in correctional facilities before either resources become available or
their case is disposed of through probation or incarceration.[cccxxx] Despite
collaboration of interested stakeholders and agencies, there are
gatekeepers for particular "silos" of treatment options. Such silos may
preclude defendants from participation unless they are incarcerated and
enter the program through DOC or CSSD.[cccxxxi] These silos and
treatment options break down as follows:

Judicial Department - Court Diversion PreTrial Services and Special Sessions

- Accelerated rehabilitation (AR) Conn. General Statutes ("C.G.S") §§54-56e
- Psychiatric AR
- Pretrial Drug Education Program- C.G.S. §54-56i
- Criminal Injuries Compensation Fund C.G.S. §54-56h
- Pretrial Supervised Diversionary Program for persons with psychiatric disabilities and veterans C.G.S. §54-56l
- Mediation Programs C.G.S. §54-56m
- Youthful Offender C.G.S. §54-76b allows for erasure
- Pretrial Alcohol Education Program (AEP) C.G.S. §54-56g
- Family Violence Education Program
- Pretrial School Violence Prevention Program C.G.S. §54-56j
- Community Service Labor program[cccxxxii]

Judicial Department - Special Court Sessions

- Community Court[cccxxxiii]
- Domestic Violence Docket
- Drug Intervention Program (Drug Court Dockets)

Department of Mental Health and Addiction Services – (DMHAS)

- Mental Health Jail Diversion
- Jail Diversion/Court Liaison Program
- Jail Diversion Substance Abuse Program
- Women's Jail Diversion Program
- Veterans' Jail Diversion and Trauma Recovery Services[cccxxxiv]
- Alternative Drug Intervention
- Pretrial Alcohol Education Program
- Pretrial Drug Education Program
- Community Recovery Engagement Support and Treatment Center - New Haven
- Advanced Supervision and Intervention Support Team/DMHAS/CSSD/DOC
- Sierra Pretrial Center - CSSD/DMHAS[cccxxxv]

Importance of Arraignment - The Critical Stage for Diversion

Pretrial incarceration and the failure to make bond is the most reliable indicator that the defendant will end up with a sentence involving incarceration.^{cccxxxvi} That is because "pretrial detention [has been] shown to have an adverse impact on the trajectory of a criminal case."^{cccxxxvii} The decision to detain a defendant pretrial or impose a monetary bond on a defendant who cannot afford to post bond is often tantamount to a decision to convict.

Fortunately, Connecticut law provides a public defender to offenders at arraignment, a practice not all states follow.^{cccxxxviii} This allows counsel to assist defendants with bail arguments and pursue an opportunity to seek diversion early in the process. In Connecticut, all public defender offices have in-house social workers who assist attorneys and indigent clients with diversion referrals to CSSD, DMHAS and other appropriate diversion programs.^{cccxxxix} Despite the opportunity for appointment of counsel and social work assistance, additional resources are needed at arraignment to make sure counsel can make an effective argument for diversion at that first appearance.

As the American Bar Association has observed, "[p]roceedings to determine pretrial release are conducted under circumstances that would not be tolerated at trial. Courtrooms may be noisy and overcrowded, and cases may be treated hurriedly in order to dispose of a large volume of cases in a short period of time....Appearances should not be conducted in a perfunctory manner. Rather, reflecting the importance of the decisions made at this stage, the proceedings should be held in physical facilities that are appropriate for the administration of justice and conducted with the dignity and decorum to be expected of a court proceeding. Each case should be treated individually, with attention to the information about the case that has been developed by the prosecutor, defense counsel and pre-trial services."^{cccxl}

In Connecticut, despite bail recommendations and guidelines, "a judge can justify almost any bond...[c]ertain judges will assess certain cases differently. You can assemble a room full of judges and the range of bail for the same crime can vary from $5,000 to $250,000. It's their individual decision."cccxli The average arraignment lasts five minutes, sometimes less. In that time, the judge gets only a snapshot of each case -- the defense's position, the prosecution's position, the police report and the bail commissioner's recommendation.cccxlii

The Cost of Failure to Make Bail or Gain Access to A Diversion Program

The Justice Policy Institute maintains that "[t]he ability to pay money bail is neither an indicator of a person's guilt nor an indicator of risk of release. The focus on money as a mechanism for pretrial release means people often are not properly screened for more rational measures of public safety. Meanwhile, those too poor to pay a money bail remain in jail regardless of their risk level or presumed innocence." cccxliii From 1992 to 2006, the use of financial release, primarily through commercial bonds, increased by 32 percent" and increased in amount by $30,000 between the same dates.cccxliv Research also shows that people who are detained pretrial and unable to make bond amounts are under added pressure to enter a guilty plea even if innocent of the charge in order to regain freedom and family.cccxlv In Connecticut more often than not, a person who is detained pretrial must wait eight months before filing a request for a speedy trial.cccxlvi

Diversion Can Mitigate, But Cannot Entirely Prevent, All Collateral Consequences of Arrest, Incarceration and Conviction

The collateral consequences of arrest can inflict damage to those arrested and their families. Many criminal court practitioners are uneducated about these consequences. Defendants similarly situated to Robert, Jocelyn and Eduardo (the defendants portrayed above) are often punished far beyond any period of incarceration that may be offered by the prosecution.[cccxlvii] Some mistakenly assume collateral consequences only occur as a result of a felony conviction.[cccxlviii] **But for many defendants, it is the mere fact of arrest or short term-incarceration that triggers the loss of employment, housing, child custody and the risk of deportation.**[cccxlix]

Research indicates that when a family member is incarcerated, the trauma is generational. Children suffer the consequences of trauma, depression, shame, loss of stable housing, separation from siblings, educational disruption, foster care and termination of parental rights. Children with an incarcerated parent are more likely to be at risk for involvement in the criminal justice system themselves.[cccl]

In 2011, the Chair of the ABA's Criminal Justice Section commented that ABA council members and criminal justice stakeholders decided that "diversion and collateral consequences were two of the most important criminal justice issues facing the justice system in the next three to five years."[cccli] It is imperative that lawmakers in Connecticut consider smart-on-crime versus tough-on-crime policies that permit a shift of resources now invested in incarceration toward the critical pre-arrest and pretrial "front end" of the criminal justice system.[ccclii] Such a shift would allow courts to make better and earlier decisions to divert defendants who can be removed safely from the criminal justice system altogether. Recognizing this landscape, we must redefine "reentry" as a process that begins at arrest and continues through community reintegration.[cccliii] After decades of focusing on the importance of re-entry, Connecticut must focus on "no-entry" as a promising alternative to incarceration.

Best Practices -- Diversion Initiatives in Other States

Washington State – Alternatives to Total Confinement for Some Parents of Minor Children.

In 2010, Washington initiated community placement as an alternative to confinement for appropriate offenders who are parents of minor children. There are actually two components of the program, one court-based and one through the Department of Corrections. The court-side program is the Family and Offender Sentencing Alternative (FOSA). The corrections program is The Community Parenting Alternative (CPA).[cccliv]

Law Enforcement Assisted Diversion (LEAD)

LEAD[ccclv] is a Seattle-based program that offers viable pre-charge alternatives to arrest and prosecution of low-level drug offenses. LEAD is a "street level" law versus court-involvement law enforcement diversion program. LEAD was created through the collaborative effort of all criminal justice stakeholders.

Oklahoma – Okla. Stat. § 22-20

Oklahoma law requires judges at sentencing to consider the effects of a parent's incarceration on children. They must inquire whether a convicted person is a custodial parent and, if so, what arrangements are available for the care of the children.[ccclvi]

Vermont – Rapid Intervention Community Court Diversion Instead of Arrest for Heroin and Opioid Addiction -- an Integration of Public Health and Public Safety

Vermont has seen statewide heroin use of epidemic proportions. But instead of incarcerating defendants, Vermont is utilizing court diversion with required treatment. The programs report that at least 80 percent of participants are drug free after one year. The Rapid Intervention Community Court has the endorsement of Chittenden State's Attorney T.J. Donovan because of its success rate. Vermont is considering legislation that would standardize such diversion programs throughout the state.ccclvii In a recent press release, U.S. Sen. Patrick Leahy of Vermont stated that, "[l]aw enforcement would rather not arrest and prosecute the same offenders over and over when the underlying issue is a treatable addiction. Treating the addiction can be the better and less costly approach. It has the added benefit of fewer cases landing on detectives' and prosecutors' desks."ccclviii

Texas

In 2007, prior to the current economic recession, Texas halted prison construction. Instead, it invested $241 million into treatment and diversion programs. The parole failure rate is down 39 percent since 2007.ccclix

Chapter 11: JUVENILE JUSTICE INITIATIVES AND IN-SCHOOL PROGRAMS

Barack, known to his friends as "Barry," was a third-year honor student at a private college preparatory school in New Haven. One week from celebrating his 17th birthday, he was convicted of cocaine possession and distribution. Upon such conviction, his life changed forever.

His father, a native Kenyan, met his mother in New Haven while attending college as a foreign student on scholarship. They were married the following year. Within a year of Barry's birth, his parents separated. His father returned to Kenya and had little contact thereafter with Barry. His mom eventually moved to Indonesia to pursue her interest in archeology. Barry chose to return to the U.S. to attend high school. He moved in with his grandparents.

Barry excelled in school. He had several Ivy League schools interested in him. All indications were he would qualify for an academic scholarship that would fully cover his tuition, room and board. He aspired to become a lawyer. He also liked to indulge in the recreational use of drugs with his friends. He was a member of the "choom gang," with whom he regularly used alcohol, marijuana and cocaine.

As part of its war on drugs, Connecticut in 1987 passed legislation imposing mandatory punishment on the possession of a ½ gram of crack cocaine.

One night in the winter of 1988, Barry's junior year, the choom gang pooled their monies to buy a gram of crack. Later that night, three members, including Barry, jumped in a car to make deliveries to the rest of the gang. The car had a busted tail light and an expired registration. The police stopped the car. After noticing a crack pipe on the backseat, they

99

conducted a search, resulting in the discovery of the crack and several ounces of marijuana. All three teens were arrested and tried as adults. They were convicted and sentenced to prison.

Upon serving his sentence, Barry lost any chance he had of a college scholarship. He searched in vain for meaningful employment. Eventually, he resorted to using hard drugs, including heroin. He has been in and out of prison all of his adult life.

The above story, while fictional, underscores a cold, harsh reality. The war on drugs has led to the imprisonment of multitudes of teenagers across two generations for crimes that qualify as youthful indiscretions. Even our current president could have fallen into this snare.ᶜᶜᶜˡˣ The consequences of incarceration are dire, not only for juveniles, but also their families and the communities in which they live.

A criminal record often slams shut the door leading to one's pursuit of the American dream and the opportunity for upward mobility.

Can we, as a nation, afford to subject yet another generation of youth to the overreach of our current criminal justice system?

Key Questions

In light of recent research on the plasticity and immaturity of the juvenile brain and the cost-effective benefits of collaborative family and school interventions, do we still believe that imprisonment is the most effective way to teach young people to be law-abiding citizens? Does it serve the public interest to channel young people into a criminal justice system that stigmatizes them with adult-size permanent criminal records and provides them with more criminal peers?

Key Observations

• <u>Myth</u>: The juvenile justice system is color-blind and gives youthful offenders a second chance to reform and turn their lives around.

• <u>Reality</u>: Connecticut is moving in the right direction. It recently raised the age for juvenile transfers to adult court. It is also providing appropriate programming for juveniles involved in criminal activity. However, more attention and funding is needed to reduce racial disparity and improve school disciplinary practices.

• Connecticut should move to discretionary, not mandatory, transfer to adult court for all juveniles involved in crime.

• Connecticut should allow improved programming and parole opportunities for juveniles sentenced to lengthy prison sentences.

• Connecticut should improve support for early childhood development, including visiting nurses for young parents, diaper banks, child care, pre-school and after-school opportunities, and focus special attention and support on children with incarcerated parents.

• Connecticut should improve trauma, addiction and mental health treatment for at-risk or abused children, both outside of and within the criminal justice system.

• Connecticut should continue to improve diagnostic practices for early detection of learning disabilities, child abuse, trauma exposure and other indicators of children at risk.

• Connecticut should continue to explore better ways to keep children in high school through graduation.

• Wrap-around and coordination of existing services (mental health, poverty, family therapy, addiction,

**education, physical health, criminal, social work) should
continue to be improved.**

The Current State of Affairs in Connecticut

In the 1990s, criminal policy experts predicted that because of
the increasing numbers of young people on the demographic horizon
and the rise of crack-related violence in the cities, we would soon
experience a juvenile crime wave. For example, criminologist James Alan
Fox predicted in 1995 that 14-17 year old offenders would commit
between 5,000 and 9,000 homicides nationally in 2004. The actual
number was less than 1,000.ccclxi State legislatures, including
Connecticut's, reacted to these dire predictions by lowering the age of
adulthood and subjecting juveniles to "adult time
for adult crime." In 1995, Connecticut passed
legislation requiring children as young as 14 to
be automatically tried and sentenced as adults if
the crime were serious enough.ccclxii

> It is more likely
> that an African-
> American boy
> who drops out of
> high school will
> be arrested than
> get a job.

At the same time, schools began to
develop "zero tolerance" programs. Student
disciplinary problems were treated with
immediate suspension or expulsion, and police were summoned for any
criminal violation at school. The newly adversarial and prosecutorial
attitude taken by school officials toward students nationwide was
exemplified by *Safford v. Redding*, a case in which a 13-year-old honor
student was stripped-searched because of allegations that she had
brought Advil to school.ccclxiii

Children who were tracked into the adult criminal justice system
were not given the counseling, education and family therapy programs
available to those in the juvenile system. Their immaturity and the social
and family circumstances that contributed to their criminal conduct were
taken into account, if at all, only inconsistently and informally in the plea
bargaining process – not in official sentencing practices. Judges were

directed by statute to sentence juveniles as though they were adults. Those juveniles who refused to plead guilty (often on advice from ill-informed friends or relatives) were entitled to receive no consideration of their youth.

We now know that this policy of treating kids as adults was not only expensive and unnecessary, but counterproductive. Studies across the country have shown that treating juveniles harshly only increases the likelihood that they will continue to commit crimes, by: (1) increasing the barriers to successful reentry, (2) "schooling" them in crime, (3) denying them the family therapy and support, educational opportunities and drug treatment programs they would have in juvenile court, and (4) denying them hope and a realistic alternative path. Because kids are among the most amenable to rehabilitation and reformation, they are also the most vulnerable to their environments, including prison settings. We waste the opportunity to turn kids around when we give them long sentences. But Connecticut now has hundreds of kids who have been permanently stigmatized by adult convictions. Four people in Connecticut are serving life-without-parole sentences for crimes they committed as children, and over 50 are serving sentences of 50 years or more.[ccclxiv]

The vast majority (75-90 percent) of children serving sentences longer than 10 years come from predominantly minority communities in Connecticut, where zero-tolerance school policies, poverty, housing instability and the criminal involvement and imprisonment of their own parents, friends and relatives (and expansive doctrines of accomplice liability) make it far too easy for a kid to end up in the criminal justice system. The national statistics are stark: It is more likely that an African-American boy who drops out of high school will be arrested than get a job.

Connecticut has begun to turn these statistics around. A strong and successful legislative campaign in 2007 (effective in 2010) to "raise the age" at which juveniles will be considered adults now means that kids aged 16 and 17 who are charged with less serious crimes will be treated in the juvenile justice system, not the adult system. Connecticut Court Support Services Division has developed evidence-based programming for juvenile offenders that has been quite successful since the "Raise the Age" law was passed. The early results from these welcome changes show that, despite the increased numbers of kids eligible for the juvenile system, the number of juveniles referred to juvenile court is down 16.5 percent. In 2009, 67 percent of juveniles started treatment programs but only 20 percent completed them. However, in 2013, 96 percent started treatment and 76 percent completed it. Twelve-month recidivism rates are down to under 50 percent for all juveniles and below 30 percent for 17-year-olds. Twenty-four-month re-arrest rates are down from 66 percent in 2007 to 56 percent in the second quarter of 2013. The rate of juvenile commitment is also down from 589 in 2003 to 198 in 2013.ccclxv **Connecticut is now a national leader in cutting juvenile commitment rates and in using evidence-based and collaborative programming to help kids find a path out of crime.**

> One Missouri study concluded that the recidivism rate could be reduced as much by 50 percent, to one out of every four ex-offenders returned to prison within two years of release, if ex-offenders were armed with a GED and a job.

The Department of Correction, like CSSD, has been taking laudable steps to recognize developmental differences and the effects of mental illness and trauma on young people. It no longer houses 14- and 15-year-olds with 16- and 17-year olds at the Manson Youth Institution. It has found that this small change reduces violence in that institution because 14- and 15-year-olds no longer react defensively to bigger, older boys. Moreover, Commissioner James E. Dzurenda investigated the heightened violence experienced in gang-segregation units over the past 10 years, closely examining the files of those responsible for violence. He found that those most often responsible for the violence were not the gang leaders, but more socially-vulnerable inmates with learning and other cognitive disabilities who were being extorted or manipulated into committing violent acts. Separating these inmates from the gang leaders, teaching them about their disabilities, and giving them strategies for avoiding manipulation and getting outside help when confronted was far more effective in cutting rates of prison violence than simply increasing the duration of imprisonment or imposing solitary confinement. We can learn lessons from these "inside" interventions about stopping violence on the outside by paying closer attention to children's mental, physical, and emotional health and environments.

Several challenges remain, however. One big challenge is the disparate impact of the criminal justice system on minority kids. Connecticut -- along with other "worst-rate" states like Louisiana, Alabama, West Virginia, Pennsylvania, Georgia, Ohio, Michigan, Minnesota, Nebraska and the Dakotas -- still imprisons minorities at four times the rate of whites.[ccclxvi] The most recent statistical evaluation of disproportionate minority contact in the juvenile justice system in Connecticut in 2009 found that this disparity is not explained by differences in the severity or frequency of minority kids' criminal conduct.[ccclxvii] The simple fact is that if a black youth and white youth commit the same crime in the same circumstances, the black youth is more likely to go to jail. CSSD is currently developing programming to address this disparity.

A second and related challenge is avoiding the "school-to-prison" pipeline. In the three-year period between 2008 and 2010, more than 22,000 Connecticut high school students left high school before graduating.[ccclxviii] Of that group, 28 percent of these "transferred" to adult education programming, but failed to complete it.

Students who are arrested at school, who are expelled to the streets, or who are diverted to adult education programs that provide less oversight are at far greater risk of falling into the criminal justice system than those who are kept in school. However, in part because minority students tend to be concentrated in under-resourced schools, minority students nationally are far more likely to be arrested or suspended than white students, and boys are far more likely to be arrested or suspended than girls.[ccclxix]

CIVIL RIGHTS DATA COLLECTION   MARCH 2012

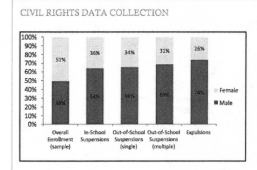

Discipline
Boys vs. Girls

While male and female students each represent about half the student population, males made up 74% of the students expelled.

A Look at Race and Gender: Out-of-School Suspensions

African-American boys and girls have higher suspension rates than any of their peers. One in five African-American boys and more than one in ten African-American girls received an out-of-school suspension.

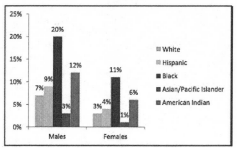

In 2010, a higher percentage of Connecticut teens enrolled *inside* DOC institutions completed GEDs (27 percent) than those enrolled in similar programs in the community (17 percent). The figures are even more dramatic for black and Latino teens: 26 percent of those enrolled in GED programs completed them in DOC, compared to 10 percent of those enrolled in the community.ccclxx One study charges that difficult students in some Connecticut schools are "encouraged" to leave high school for adult education programming or alternative high schools. This decision to transfer is racially skewed: Black students "transfer" at twice the rate of whites, and Latinos at triple the rate of whites.ccclxxi While DOC may be proud of its comparatively high GED completion rates, the high rate of high school dropouts in Connecticut, and the low rate of GED completion in the community, only expand the school-to-prison pipeline.

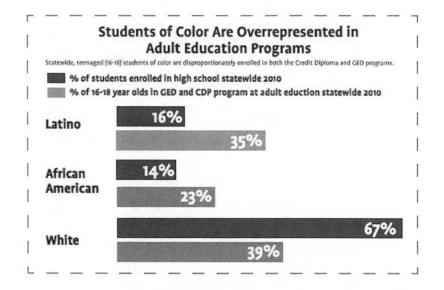

The Connecticut Office of Policy and Management, through the Juvenile Justice Advisory Committee, has been working with schools to reduce reliance on police and increase the ability of schools to deal with disciplinary matters on site.ccclxxii CSSD also recommends expansion of educational support and vocational opportunities through the schools that will allow at-risk kids to find a path to a steady job and better life.

A third challenge is how we respond to the mistaken policies of the past. Many children prosecuted in the harsh days of the 1990s as adults are still serving life-equivalent sentences in Connecticut. Many of these cases are not currently eligible for parole, despite Supreme Court decisions that require most juveniles to be given "a meaningful chance" at parole. The Supreme Court emphasized that children have limited control over their living situations, have (as all children do) impulsive and immature judgment, but at the same time, have an increased ability to change and reform.ccclxxiii

Connecticut still retains an "automatic transfer" law that requires 14-17 year olds to be prosecuted as adults for certain serious crimes, regardless of the circumstances and without any judicial discretion. Many other states have "discretionary transfer" laws that give judges some discretion to take the circumstances of the crime into account before transferring a juvenile to adult court. **A 2008 meta-analysis by the U.S. Department of Justice's Office of Juvenile Justice and Delinquency Prevention found little evidence that automatic transfer statutes deterred juvenile crime. However, in several well-designed studies, treating juvenile offenders as adults, especially in cases of violent crime, increased their recidivism rates by as much as 100 percent , compared with treating them as juveniles.**cclxxiv

Automatic transfer statutes also ignore the effects of trauma and abuse on children. A national survey of juveniles serving life-without-parole sentences found that 80 percent had witnessed violence at home and many were themselves victims of abuse.cclxxv Fifty-four percent had witnessed violence in their neighborhoods *every week*. Recent research into childhood trauma has found that chronic, pervasive, environmental violence, such as living in a violent home or neighborhood, can lead children to cope by resorting to indifference, defiance, or aggression to protect themselves or other loved ones. But with appropriate treatment for trauma, children can regain trust in others and develop more control over trauma-triggered behaviors.cclxxvi

As one man who is currently serving a long sentence in Connecticut for juvenile criminal behavior recalled: **"My mom used to beat me ... I got tired ... I wanted to get the hell out of there. But there's nowhere to go. ... My cousin got killed right in front of me when I was 13 or 14 years old...hurt real bad. [I was so broke down afterwards that my mother called 9-1-1 and the hospital] did some tests, asked questions, and I stayed a night or two ... That stuck with me. Made me feel like guns would protect me, and I needed protection."**cclxxvii

However, despite thoughtful changes by DOC, and even with far better programming than is currently available, the adult court and prison environments are more likely to exacerbate trauma triggers than to help victimized young people to understand and overcome them. The recidivism statistics demonstrate that treating violent juvenile offenders through the

juvenile system rather than the adult system whenever possible is more likely to improve recidivism and long-term public safety than longer and longer prison sentences.

Connecticut has not yet passed a law that would comply with Supreme Court decisions and give juveniles who were sentenced to decades-long sentences a shot at demonstrating they have grown up and changed. House Bill 5221, which would allow a chance for parole in these cases after 60 percent of the sentence is served, was under consideration by the Legislature.

Best Practices

Juveniles have the **best** prospects for reform and change. The earlier we involve juveniles in positive programs, the better the prospects of keeping them out of the criminal justice system. Here are some of the evidence-based reforms from other jurisdictions[ccclxxviii] that are cost-effective and work:

- Home nurse visits for young mothers

- Diaper programs and child care availability for young mothers

- Head Start pre-school programs

- School lunch programs

- After-school homework help programs

- Family and school wrap-around counseling and therapy

- In-school discipline, rather than expulsion or arrest

- Early diagnosis and treatment of learning and mental disabilities, trauma and abuse

- Broadly available education and vocational training

• Addiction services for youth; diversion for drug crimes

• Educational, mental health, drug treatment, and family programming in juvenile facilities

• Discretionary transfer to adult court rather than mandatory transfer, with trained juvenile court personnel making the transfer decision rather than line prosecutors or adult court judges

• Training of all school and police personnel on disparate impact and cultural sensitivity

• Preserving children's ties, when possible and productive, with incarcerated parents and extended family

• Strengthening positive social ties for young people through mentorship and family counseling programs

• Providing counseling and material and emotional support for children with incarcerated parents

Chapter 12: GOALS AND RECOMMENDATIONS

The preceding review of our state's criminal justice system and incarceration practices reveals that Connecticut lags well behind those states that have been lauded as models in a number of categories, including recidivism, system costs and the percentage of population either in prison or under supervision. It is imperative that Connecticut utilize some of the more effective models and practices seen in other states or countries.

In recent years, the state and Department of Correction have made progress in stabilizing Connecticut's prison population, somewhat reducing recidivism, implementing meaningful juvenile justice reform, adopting probation and parole revocation reforms, and passing the Justice Reinvestment Act in 2009.

Nonetheless, the pace of reform has been excruciatingly slow. There are opportunities to slash costs, speed reform and improve the process of administering the criminal justice system in Connecticut without imperiling public safety. These changes would enable the system to function better at lower cost, provide effective addiction and mental illness therapies, and deliver fairer justice.

All segments of the system need to be addressed. At the front end (arraignment and pre-sentencing), we need to right-size our prisons by (1) re-evaluating those crimes that warrant incarceration versus other forms of retribution and (2) reducing the length of sentences and prison stays, particularly for non-violent crimes, minor drug violations, technical parole violators and DUI offenses. At the same time, we should explore reforms that promote fairer treatment of minors, the drug-addicted and the mentally-challenged. The mid-point of the system (incarceration) needs more scrutiny in terms of overcrowding, excessive use of solitary confinement and the need for more proven, evidence-based addiction, anger management, drug and mental health therapies and treatments. Connecticut needs to make educational and job training programs more broadly and effectively available. The end of the process (re-entry) has significant opportunities for meaningful improvement, including reform of probation and parole violations and the adoption of alternative punishments in lieu of re-incarceration, a commitment to the creation of more job opportunities for former offenders, the elimination of restrictions on the availability of public assistance, and more adequate funding of social service agencies that fulfill a significant level of the state's responsibilities for recently-released offenders.

To its credit, Connecticut has already embarked on a number of the recommendations we advocate. That being said, it could pursue such reforms more vigorously and with far greater speed. It still lags significantly behind other states. Delaware serves as an example of how quickly reform can occur and yield benefits. See Chapter 14.

Effecting a series of changes to laws, policies and practices is more likely to succeed with clearly defined goals and outcomes in mind. Such goals should drive the selection of specific reform measures.

Desired Outcomes

In our collective view, the four most significant goals or priorities to be pursued are straightforward and non-controversial:

1. Reduce Connecticut's prison population, especially non-violent offenders who pose a low risk to public safety, by half within five years;

2. Reduce Connecticut's recidivism rate by 30 percentage points or more within 5 years;

3. Close half of the state's correctional facilities within 5 years; and

4. Reduce state spending on the prison system by half in five years, with two-thirds of the savings redirected to proven evidence-based drug and mental health treatments, educational and vocational training and post-release support and supervision programs.

Recommendations

Based on our review of the best practices in other states and countries, we have developed a set of 30 recommendations that will help realize the four desired outcomes. We have grouped our 30 recommendations into five categories: Legislative Changes; Executive Policies and Practices; Department of Correction Initiatives; Alternatives to Incarceration; and Improvement in the Re-entry Process.

Legislative Changes

Recommendation No. 1

Enactment of legislative reforms to reduce the use of long-term minimum mandatory sentences for non-violent offenses and/or prisoners who do not pose a high risk to public safety, and/or to allow for the exercise of discretion and consideration of the actual history of violent behavior or propensity for violence of offenders (including elimination of the inflexible requirement to serve 85 percent of a sentence in all cases of crimes classified as "violent").

Recommendation No. 2

Enactment of legislative reforms aimed at vesting judges with greater discretion relative to sentencing and sentencing conditions, including the use of an offender-based data system, sentencing-support analytics and mandatory offender family impact statements to facilitate informed decision-making.

Recommendation No. 3

Adoption of legislative and/or executive reforms to provide parole and probation officers with greater discretion in handling parole/probation violations.

Recommendation No. 4

Adoption of legislative and/or executive reforms to enhance the prospects of early parole and time off for good behavior.

Recommendation No. 5

Enactment of legislative and executive reforms aimed at reducing parole and probation revocations and minimizing re-incarceration for minor or technical parole or probation violations.

Recommendation No. 6

Creation of tax and other incentives to encourage in-state employers to hire ex-offenders.

Recommendation No. 7

Provide some protection and civil immunity to employers who hire ex-offenders.

Executive Policies and Practices

Recommendation No. 8

Formation of a cabinet-level committee to coordinate legislative and executive reforms, whose members are drawn from high-level state agency executives, the state attorney general's office, law enforcement, mental health and drug rehabilitation service providers, prisoner advocacy groups, victims' rights advocates, faith-based groups and local community organizations.

Recommendation No. 9

Take full advantage of the Bureau of Justice Assistance's Justice Reinvestment Initiative (JRI) recidivism programs and the National Institute of Corrections' Transition from Prison to Community Model projects.

Recommendation No. 10

Allocation of one-third of the cost savings realized from the reduction of prison beds and the closure of correctional facilities toward GED and other educational programs and vocational training aimed at reducing recidivism and enhancing the employment prospects of releasees.

Recommendation No. 11

Allocation of one-third of the cost savings from the reduction in the number of prison beds and the closure of correctional facilities toward proven evidence-based treatment and post-release support programs.

Recommendation No. 12

> Allocate the remaining one-third by giving 30 percent of the cost savings from the reduction of prison beds and the closure of correctional facilities to the General Fund as a taxpayer dividend and give 3 percent of such cost savings to a newly-created victims' fund to pay for counseling and treatment of victims and educational scholarships for the family members of victims.

Recommendation No. 13

> Sell mothballed prison properties and earmark the sale proceeds for housing vouchers, additional halfway houses, the expansion of mental health facilities and treatment options and the funding of the pension liabilities of corrections personnel. Strong consideration should be given to converting one or more correctional facilities into mental health hospitals, thereby redressing the acute shortage of such facilities in our state.

Recommendation No. 14

> Place a freeze on both the hiring of correctional officers and the authorization of overtime, so as to align the size of the correctional force with the reduced number of inmates and prisons. Also re-train existing correctional officers to provide post-release supervision services, including as parole and probation officers.

Department of Correction Initiatives

Recommendation No. 15

> Development of an accurate and detailed offender database (accessible by all state agencies and

stakeholders) and procurement of proven analytical tools to assist judges in analyzing, on both an aggregated and individualized basis, criminal histories and propensity for violence in connection with arraignment, pretrial release and sentencing matters.

Recommendation No. 16

Procurement of additional proven analytical tools for assessing prisoner treatment needs and risks.

Recommendation No. 17

Procurement of proven analytical tools to assist probation and parole authorities in setting and supervising parole and probation conditions.

Recommendation No. 18

Expand the number of mental health professionals on staff at correctional facilities and re-train current correctional staff members to enable them to provide and/or support mental health services.

Recommendation No. 19

For women offenders, implement holistic, trauma-influenced, gender-appropriate counseling and treatment programs.

Recommendation No. 20

Development of a set of proven, evidence-based, alternative post-release sanctions that can be administered quickly and decisively in lieu of parole revocations and re-incarceration.

Recommendation No. 21

Development of an accurate and detailed offender

database (accessible by all state agencies and stakeholders) and procurement of proven analytical tools for (a) measuring recidivism on both an aggregated and individualized basis and (b) more effectively tracking offenders following their release.

Recommendation No. 22

Expand the use of parole and supervised release for ex-offenders as a way of both enhancing public safety and increasing the prospects of rehabilitation.

Incarceration Alternatives and No-Entry Diversion Programs

Recommendation No. 23

As an overall guiding principle, substitute treatment for incarceration in the case of addicted, mentally ill and DUI offenders, particularly where they do not pose an inordinate threat to public safety.

Recommendation No. 24

Condition expungement of criminal arrests or convictions on the successful completion of diversion programs and staying clean.

Recommendation No. 25

Examine ways to reduce the stigma or collateral consequence of criminal arrests for those defendants placed in diversionary programs.

Recommendation No. 26

> In connection with arraignments, pretrial release and consideration of referrals to diversion programs, require the submission and consideration of family impact statements.

Improving the Re-entry Process

Recommendation No. 27

> Double inmate GED graduation rates and vocational training completion rates every two years and condition participation in such programs on sustained good behavior.

Recommendation No. 28

> Mandatory and/or greater use of individual Transitional Accountability Plans (TAPs) for prisoners entering the correctional system with parole eligibility. Implementation and/or greater use of Transitional Housing Units (THUs) for prisoners who possess a high risk of recidivism.

Recommendation No. 29

> Appoint a commission to examine possible measures to reduce the stigma, loss of entitlements and/or other collateral impediments facing prisoners upon their release (including in the housing and job markets).

Recommendation No. 30

> Development and/or greater use of proven, evidence-based, post-release support programs (e.g., job counseling/training, housing vouchers) that can be incorporated as part of TAPs and THUs.

• Bernice moved to Mary Magdalene House from York Correctional Institution after doing 10 years. Intensely faith-focused, Bernice now works at a Fortune 500 company. She wants to get her own place and be with her family.

Chapter 13: WILL REFORM THREATEN THE SAFETY OF CONNECTICUT CITIZENS?

When one raises the specter of reform aimed at diverting offenders, right-sizing our prisons and facilitating re-entry, the first reaction of many law-abiding citizens understandably is focused on the highly charged emotional question: "WILL I AND MY FAMILY BE PLACED AT GREATER RISK?"

Without being able to answer this question in the negative, the prospects for enacting reform and effecting a meaningful cut in our prison population likely vanish.

In the face of this political reality, the editors of this book have endeavored to keep the public safety implications of reform top-of-mind in assessing the wisdom of alternative approaches to incarceration. In our consideration of "best practices" and in making specific recommendations, we have rigorously considered whether adoption of a specific practice or approach would place the public at greater risk of physical harm. If, in our collective judgment, the answer was yes, we eliminated any such practice or approach from further consideration.

We believe, with a high degree of confidence, that adoption of each of our recommendations will not jeopardize the public. Our belief is rooted, in large part, in the experience of other states that have implemented prison or sentencing reforms and/or right-sized their prison populations, including most notably New York. New York has achieved a significant reduction in its prison population over the past decade, while reducing the level of criminal activity, including violent crime rates.

Relevant statistics in Connecticut strongly suggest that a dramatic cut in the number of incarcerated individuals can be realized at no cost in terms of public safety. Indeed, reform, if carried out properly, may yield improvements in public safety, particularly in urban areas where the overwhelming majority of violent crime occurs in Connecticut (i.e., Hartford, New Haven, Bridgeport and Waterbury). In suburban communities, one would not expect an undue adverse impact from the reforms recommended herein. The taxpayers in such communities would likely realize tax relief and/or better results for their hard-earned tax dollars.

So what are the statistics that support our belief that prison and criminal justice reform will not come at a cost to public safety? We rely on the following data points:

(1) after explosive growth from 1980 to 2008, Connecticut's prison population is down 16 percent since 2008;

(2) violent crime in Connecticut is down 8 percent since 2008;

(3) property crime in our state is down 8 percent since 2008;

(4) total arrests are down 19 percent since 2008;

(5) Connecticut is among the safest states in the U.S., with the seventh-lowest crime rate in the country;

(6) among the nine Northeastern States, Connecticut has the third lowest crime rate (behind New Jersey and New York);

(7) despite the fact it is a relatively safe state, Connecticut's incarceration rate (333 per 100,000) is the second-highest among the nine Northeastern states (trailing only Pennsylvania);

(8) Connecticut's incarceration rate is well above those of New Jersey (261) and New York (276);

(9) Connecticut's incarceration rate of 333 per 100,000 puts it in the upper third nationally;

(10) while Connecticut has seen its recidivism rate decline somewhat since 2005, it remains relatively high.[ccclxxix]

(11) Recently, Connecticut has substantially reformed its juvenile justice system by (a) drastically reducing the number of juveniles in detention facilities despite raising the age at which offenders are categorized as juvenile from 16 to 18 and (b) pouring the savings therefrom into evidence-based community "treatment and support programs,"[ccclxxx]

(12) As a consequence of the foregoing reforms, juvenile crime rates, arrests and recidivism have all declined;[ccclxxxi] and

(13) The foregoing juvenile justice results have been realized at no added annual cost to the state's budget.[ccclxxxii]

As chronicled in the preceding chapters, the foregoing statistics underscore that Connecticut's incarceration rate is out of alignment with the current threat levels to public safety. This amounts to hyper-incarceration. This conclusion is drawn from an incontestable fact: The explosive growth in Connecticut's prison population since the 1980s has been driven not by an increase in violent crime, but rather by a dramatic spike in non-violent, drug-related arrests, coupled with longer mandatory minimum sentences and lengthier prison stays.

Faced with prison overcrowding, Connecticut state legislators and correction officials in 2004 recognized the "over-correction" that had occurred. In 2004, Connecticut became the first state to enact "justice reinvestment" reforms aimed at reducing overcrowding and reinvesting the savings therefrom in treatment and other rehabilitative programs. At the time, Connecticut was lauded as a "pioneer" at the cutting edge of reform.

However, Connecticut's standing as a progressive state on prison "right-sizing" proved to be short-lived. Connecticut's path toward meaningful reform was side-tracked, in part, by the horrific tragedy that occurred in Cheshire in 2007. On July 23, 2007, two ex-convicts, while out on supervised parole, invaded the Cheshire home of Dr. William Petit. They beat Dr. Petit with a baseball bat and tied him up in the basement. They proceeded upstairs. They tied up his wife and 11- and 17-year-old daughters. Eventually, they sexually assaulted the mother and the 11-year-old. They later burned the house down, killing the mother and both daughters. Dr. Petit managed to escape. The two ex-cons, Steven Hayes and Joshua Komisarjevsky, were tried, convicted and sentenced to death. They remain incarcerated to this day.ccclxxxiii

Following the tragedy, Connecticut's then-Governor, Jodi Rell, essentially froze parole. Connecticut's prison population spiked to almost 20,000. Thereafter, Connecticut's reform efforts slowed in sharp contrast to New York. Cheshire heightened public fear. The Cheshire tragedy, while seven years old, remains indelibly etched in the minds of most of our citizens.

That said, we believe Cheshire should not impede reforms that are focused on curtailing or shortening incarceration for offenders who have not committed heinous violent crimes and do not pose a likely risk of violent behavior. Prisons should be a place predominantly reserved for those offenders who, as a consequence of their actions and history of violent behavior, pose a serious threat to public safety. Currently, Connecticut's system of corrections employs analytical tools that assess the needs and risks to institutional security posed by everyone entering the system. Offenders are graded on a 1 – 5 scale. This rating is not an assessment of the risk posed by an offender to the public upon his or her release.

For those guilty of heinous crimes, those with a propensity for violence and those who pose as unacceptable risk to the public, we do not advocate more lenient treatment or more liberal parole availability. However, the segment of Connecticut's prison population that falls within such high-risk category is, by all indications, a distinct minority. Our suggested reforms are targeted toward the majority of prisoners whose rehabilitation prospects would be enhanced by diversionary programs and alternative treatment initiatives. As evidenced by the successes achieved by Connecticut's juvenile justice reforms, such programs, even if partially successful, have the potential to further reduce crime and promote public safety. Empirical evidence shows that a reduction in the prison population and reinvestment of the costs saved thereby in treatment programs and increased post-release supervision of high-risk offenders pays dividends in the form of lowered recidivism and enhanced public safety. Put simply, the reforms we recommend <u>do not</u> come at a cost to public safety.

At the same time, we recognize that no system is perfect. Even with mandatory minimum sentences and longer prison terms, well over 95 percent of inmates return to society. It is not possible to prevent every tragedy. Our reforms are aimed at enhancing treatment and supervision of inmates so that upon their nearly inevitable release they pose less of a risk to the public. In the case of the Cheshire tragedy, neither Hayes nor Komisarjevsky were viewed as a high risk for violence. Hayes was classified as a "minimal violence offender," despite three convictions involving illegal weapons and an escape from a halfway house. He was also cited on 23 different occasions for misconduct while incarcerated. Hayes spent over 25 years behind bars while racking up nearly 30 arrests.[ccclxxxiv] His parole was revoked twice. Hayes had completed his required sentence for third-degree burglary. Komisarjevsky similarly had served his mandatory time for twelve counts of second- and third-degree burglary. Hayes was released two months prior to the home invasion, while Komisarjevsky had been released four months prior to the Cheshire incident. When admitted on May 5, 2003, as an accused offender, Hayes was classified as an overall 3 security risk. Upon his release four years later, he was rated an overall 2. Komisarjevsky was rated as an overall 4 upon his admittance in March 2002. Upon his release five years later, he was classified as an overall 1.[ccclxxxv] This rating pertains to the risk they posed to security within the prison environment.

> Prisons should be a place predominantly reserved for those offenders who, as a consequence of their actions and history of violent behavior, pose a serious threat to public safety.

Our suggested reforms are not intended to make it easier for someone with a record of repeated violent offenses and bad behavior while in prison, such as Hayes, to be released early or receive lenient treatment. At the same time, it should be recognized that such individuals in the overwhelming majority of cases will eventually be released. Given that fact, the public is best served by a system that endeavors to treat such individuals' mental illnesses, addictions and behavioral problems and subjects them to heightened post-release supervision. Our reforms are intended to increase the odds of favorable outcomes for both the public and prisoners alike.

We strongly recommend the development of an accurate and highly detailed offender database. Such database must contain full information relative to an offender's criminal history, propensity for violence, mental and health history, behavioral record while behind bars, treatment record, parole and probation history, educational background, family history and employment record. This database must be accessible by all state officials and persons called upon to make decisions relative to sentencing, pretrial release, parole, probation, treatment and supervision (both within and outside prison walls). Such decisions must be informed and guided by comprehensive empirical evidence and state-of-the-art analytical tools. Only then is the risk to public safety fully protected.

The offender database must also allow state officials to track, analyze and evaluate on an aggregated basis all aspects of our criminal justice system. It should yield vital statistics on recidivism, parole violations, parole revocations, probation violations, probation revocations, prison sentences, length of prison stays, percentage of prisoners in jail or prison awaiting pretrial or sentencing, percentage of inmates in prison for technical parole violations, the efficacy of specific treatments, the results of no-entry programs and the performance of re-entry programs.

Our recommendations also take account of the fact that (1) the majority of new offenders entering the correctional system are young adults and (2) prisons are viewed by many experts as a breeding or training ground for further criminal behavior upon release. To stem the tide of younger offenders, we have endeavored to identify preventative approaches and school programs that may divert youth from a heretofore all-too predictable path toward incarceration, recidivism and the dire life-long collateral social and economic consequences that befall most convicts.

• Inmates seek better lives through a class at Osborne Correctional Institution. The poster allegorically speaks of the "art of reparing porcelain. ... It is understood that the repaired piece is even more beautiful than the original. The repaired piece is not considered damaged in any way."

Chapter 14: DARE TO BE GREAT, CONNECTICUT – THE IMPERATIVE TO ACT

Connecticut -- which not long ago was seen as a pioneer for needed reform -- can again lead the way toward the creation of a fiscally-responsible, far more effective, compassionate system of criminal justice and corrections.

To do so requires courage on the part of our elected representatives and appointed state officials. We challenge them and ourselves to be great. We dare all Connecticut citizens to lead the nation in charting a more effective, safe and compassionate course. A course that will serve the interests of all Connecticut citizens, young and old, male and female, rich and poor, urban and suburban, black, white and Hispanic.

Anyone who doubts that Connecticut cannot speed up its right-sizing and reform efforts need only look at what Delaware has accomplished over the past two years.

In 2011, Delaware was faced with a crisis -- budget shortfalls, a rising crime rate and overcrowded and costly prisons. Delaware ranked fourth in the nation in violent crimes.[ccclxxxvi] Its arrest rate was one in 332, as compared with the national average of one in 529.[ccclxxxvii] So how did Delaware respond? First, it applied to participate in U.S. Justice Department's Justice Reinvestment Initiative or JRI program.[ccclxxxviii] Second, its governor convened a task force in July of 2011 to study the state's criminal justice system and identify ways to reduce its inmate population, generate cost-savings, increase public safety and reduce recidivism.[ccclxxxix] On the strength of the JRI initiative, the work of the task force and a critical assessment conducted by the Vera Institute of Justice, Delaware passed legislation in June 2012, less than one year after the governor's formation of the task force.

The new law overhauled the state's criminal justice system.[cccxc]
The legislative and policy changes were focused on (1) reducing
Delaware's large pretrial and pre-sentence prison population by allowing
for supervised release of those who did not pose an undue risk to public
safety (such low-risk pretrial group took up 14 percent of the state's
prison beds in 2010)[cccxci], (2) drastically curtailing the re-incarceration of
offenders who were merely guilty of technical probation violations (who
collectively occupied 13 percent of the state's prison beds in 2010)[cccxcii],
(3) reducing the length of prison stays (the average length of prison
terms in Delaware was three years, as compared with the national
average of two years), and (4) increasing the use of evidence-based best
practices, including implementation of pretrial risk assessments,
adoption of appropriate responses to supervision violations short of re-
incarceration, and the expanded use of programs that addressed the
treatment needs of offenders and enhanced their prospects of successful
re-entry. The task force projected that its suggested reforms could
reduce the prison population by 18 percent and save over $27 million
within five years, which monies could be reinvested in the state's efforts
to lower recidivism and increase public safety.[cccxciii]

There is, in our view, no justifiable reason why Connecticut
cannot act with similar speed to adopt and carry out similar reforms.
Indeed, it is imperative that we do so.

There are a number of ways for individuals to become
meaningfully involved in bringing about favorable changes to
Connecticut's criminal justice system. For example:

-- **Share the information in this book with others;**

-- **Buy a copy of this book and give it to someone;**

-- **Write, telephone, email or visit your elected officials and
insist on change and voice your support for specific
legislative proposals;**

-- **Volunteer with social service agencies involved with
inmates, former offenders and their families -- most**

organizations in this field are under-resourced and would welcome volunteers;

-- Write Letters to the Editor and Op-Ed pieces for newspapers and other media;

-- Identify fraternal, church, civic, industry and other groups that might be receptive to presentations about the Connecticut's criminal justice system and incarceration practices; and

-- Hire qualified ex-offenders.

The single most impactful change would be to break down existing barriers and make it easier for ex-offenders to get jobs. The ongoing stigma of convicted felons and the collateral obstacles they face upon their release from prison often effectively preclude them from the job market. Understandably, many employers who hire former offenders do not acknowledge it publicly. Consequently, we do not have many high-profile employers of former offenders to serve as role models.

As a society, we need to acknowledge there are about 7,000 offenders being released to our communities in Connecticut each year. Do we want former offenders in our communities with jobs or without jobs? Do we want to place former offenders in a position to succeed? To become breadwinners? To become responsible parents? And to give back to their communities by serving as role models, particularly to young offenders?

Having a job shortly after release from prison is the key determinant of whether a former offender will return to prison or not. Aside from being self-supportive, the pride and personal satisfaction of having a job adds considerably to their successful re-integration into the community.

This is not to suggest that former offenders be given preferential treatment, but rather that qualified ex-offenders be given the same opportunity for consideration of employment as others. By qualified, we mean offenders working with a competent social service agency such as Career Resources Inc. in Bridgeport, which is focused on workforce training and development for disadvantaged and low-income jobseekers.

Employment applications that specifically inquire about arrests or felony convictions (particularly non-violent ones) significantly impede the hiring of former offenders. "Checking the Box" frequently ends the employment process, irrespective of other qualifications (including education and vocational training received while incarcerated).

For the betterment of society, employers need to re-evaluate policies and practices that restrict hiring former offenders, most of whom, as we have noted herein, are non-violent offenders posing a low risk to the public.

We understand that not all former offenders are ideal candidates for employment upon re-entry in the community. Nonetheless, many are "qualified" for employment, including those who successfully dealt with addictions, anger management and other personal issues, those who continue to be positively engaged with a social service agency's re-entry program, those who are a part of a faith-based community, and, where appropriate, those who have participated in a restorative justice program, which has offenders accept responsibility for their actions and make amends through restitution and community service. Employers, particularly smaller ones, can benefit considerably when there is a social services agency proactively involved with both former offenders and management.

There is considerable anecdotal evidence supporting the proposition that former offenders often perform better than or at least as well as other employees in terms of their work ethic, company loyalty and overall job performance. Perhaps because it is more difficult for former offenders to get a job, they are frequently more appreciative of the opportunity. Their motivation to keep the job and avoid unemployment is often striking. For many, the job they find upon re-entry represents their best and last opportunity to succeed in life.

Continuing to systematically ostracize ex-cons is simply not in society's best interest. Other countries' success in re-integrating offenders into the community demonstrates that rehabilitation and a better life is possible at no additional cost to public safety.

Connecticut is faced with the opportunity to revolutionize our country's prevailing punitive approach to corrections and adopt a model focused on rehabilitation and social integration, more akin to that prevailing in Western Europe. Connecticut's recent success in reforming its juvenile justice system affirms that the time for such a change is now.

Dare to be great! Act on the Justice Imperative!

APPENDIX – Suggested Reading Materials

Noteworthy Books, Publications, Web Sites, Blogs and Films

1. Connecticut Office of Policy and Management website:
   http://www.ct.gov/opm/criminaljustice/research

2. Pew Center on the States website:
   http://www.pewstates.org/research/reports

3. Pew Trusts website: http://www.pewtrusts.org

4. "Approaches to Reducing Recidivism: Model State Survey," published by the Criminal Justice Clinic at Yale Law School, May 2013.

5. Michelle Alexander, *The New Jim Crow: Mass Incarceration in the Age of Colorblindness* (New Press 2012)

6. Justice Research and Policy website: http://www.jrsa.metapress.com

7. "Collateral Costs: Incarceration's Effect on Economic Mobility," Pew Charitable Trusts, 2010 (Washington, D.C.) (available at: www.economicmobility.org)

8. Bruce Western and Becky Pettit, "Incarceration and Social Inequality" (available at: http://www.amacad.org/publications/doeables/10_summer_western.pdf)

9. The Sentencing Project:
   http://www.sentencingproject.org/template/index.cfm

10. The Vera Institute: http://www.vera.org

11. Right on Crime: http://www.rightoncrime.org

12. Families Against Mandatory Minimums: http://famm.org

13. Fair Sentencing For Youth: http://www.fairsentencingforyouth.org

14. Equal Justice Initiative: http://eji.org

15. Sentencing Law and Policy Blog: http://sentencing.typepad.com/

16. The Innocence Project: http://www.innocenceproject.org

17. Washington State Institute for Public Policy:
    http://www.wsipp.wa.gov/topic.asp?cat=10&subcat=0&dteslo
    t=0

18. Council of State Governments' Justice Center:
    http://asgjusticecenter.org/

19. Connecticut Department of Correction Website:
    http://www.ct.gov/doc/

20. Connecticut Reentry Roundtable Collective: http://ctreentry.info/

21. "The Future of Parole as a Key Partner in Assuring Public Safety," from
    the series *Parole Essentials: Practical Guides for Parole
    Leaders*; U.S. Department of Justice: National Institute of
    Corrections, July 2011 (available at
    http://static.nicic.gov/library/024201.pdf)

22. "Juvenile Justice Reform in Connecticut: How Collaboration and
    Commitment Have Improved Public Safety and Outcomes for
    Youths," published by the Justice Policy Institute, Washington,
    D.C. (2013).

23. Connecticut Public Television: "The Color of Justice," a documentary
    film about racial disparity in the criminal justice system in
    Connecticut. http://www.cpbn.org/program/color-justice

24. "Mothers of Bedford," a documentary about the imprisoned mothers who participated in a successful prison nursery program in Bedford, New York. http://worldchannel.org/programs/episode/mothers-of-bedford/

25. National Institute of Corrections. http://nicic.gov/

26. National Association of Sentencing Commissions. http://thenasc.org/

27. American Bar Association:

> Racial Justice Improvement Project. http://racialjusticeproject.weebly.com/index.html

> Criminal Justice: State Policy Implementation Project. http://www.americanbar.org/groups/criminal_justice/spip.html

> "Juvenile Justice: The State of Juvenile Justice 2013." http://meetings.abanet.org/webupload/commupload/CR2000 00/otherlinks_files/jj_scj2013.pdf

28. American Probation and Parole Association. Publications. https://www.appanet.org/eweb/DynamicPage.aspx?WebCod e=VC_FreePubsReports

29. National Institute on Drug Abuse. Justice Initiatives. http://www.drugabuse.gov/researchers/justice-system-research-initiatives

30. American Correctional Association. Research Notes. https://woodcarving/research/notes.asp

31. Jonathan Simon, *Governing Through Crime: How the War on Crime Transformed American Democracy and Created a Culture of Fear,* Oxford University Press, January 2007. (Available through Amazon Digital Services.)

32. Robert A. Ferguson, Inferno: An Anatomy of American Punishment, Harvard University Press, February 2014

Acknowledgement

This publication was a collaborative undertaking led by The Malta Justice Initiative. What is rather unusual is the participation of more than 30 professionals comprising our Editorial Board, each of whom has endorsed the book's content. They have been involved with most aspects of the criminal justice system in Connecticut. They are people of all faiths. They include elected officials, college and law school professors, current or former officials at the Department of Correction, representatives of law enforcement, attorneys, business and civic leaders, social service agency professionals and members of faith-based communities involved with the reentry process.

It is hoped that our collective voice will lend credibility to the issues raised herein and change perceptions about a segment of our society whose welfare is too important to ignore. We are heartened that there are viable alternative approaches and initiatives underway in Connecticut and elsewhere.

Special Thanks

We are indebted to the long hours of help provided by our team of word processors: Michael Briney; Sharon Jones-Leslie; Tama MacKay; and Suzan Miller. We also express our gratitude to Robinson + Cole LLP for providing assistance to us as part of its *pro bono* outreach program.

We would also like to thank the law students at Quinnipiac University Law School who, under the direction of Professors Linda Ross Meyer and Jennifer Herbst, donated their time to cite-check the citations and references in the book, and express our gratitude to research assistant Michael T. Palumbo.

About the Malta Justice Initiative

The Malta Justice Initiative (MJI) is a sponsored work of the Order of Malta. Prison ministry is the core mission of MJI. MJI provides support, including visitation and instruction, to the incarcerated to help them lead faith-focused and productive lives.

MJI is a separate 501(c)(3) not-for-profit corporation. It is subject to general oversight by the Order of Malta. The Order of Malta -- technically The Sovereign Military Hospitaller Order of St. John of Jerusalem of Rhodes and of Malta -- is one of the oldest institutions of Western and Christian civilization. The Order constitutes the sole unbroken continuation of the order of the Hospital of St. John, recognized in 1113. Present in Palestine in around 1050 to provide medical care for pilgrims to the Holy Land, it is a lay religious order. Its 13,500 members are devoted to the exercise of Christian virtue and charity. The Order provides assistance to the poor and the suffering. The Order of Malta is a sovereign subject under international law, with its own constitution, passports, stamps and public institutions. Today, the Order carries out its charitable works in over 120 countries and does so without regard for religion, race, gender or national origin.

www.TheJusticeImperative.org

About the Author

Brian E. Moran is a partner in the law firm of Robinson + Cole LLP. He is a civil litigator specializing in antitrust, intellectual property, licensing and other commercial disputes.

He has co-written two business books, "The Executive's Antitrust Guide To Pricing: Understanding Implications of Typical Marketing, Distribution and Pricing Practices" (2013), published by Thomson Reuters, and "E-Counsel: The Executive's Legal Guide to Electronic Commerce" (2000).

He is the founder of The Success Foundation, a non-profit that has run summer study programs on college campuses for low-income ninth graders with college potential. In 2006, the Foundation's Students Undertaking College Career Enhancing Study Skills™ Program received a Gold CQIA Innovation Prize from The Connecticut Quality Improvement Award Partnership, Inc. CQIA is Connecticut's Malcolm Baldrige National Quality Award Partner.

Mr. Moran received a B.A. with distinction from the University of Virginia and a J.D. degree from the University of Richmond School of Law.

Mark Hurley, Park City Law Center, Litigation Director; former State Prosecutor

Babz Rawls Ivy, Inner-City News, Managing Editor and Liaison, Corporate Affairs, Penfield Communications; Deacon, Church of the Redeemer, New Haven, Conn; Certified Spiritual Director; National Urban Fellow

Rev. Marilyn B. Kendrix, Church of the Redeemer, Associate Pastor; University of New Haven, Adjunct Professor

A. Stephen Lanza, Family ReEntry, Executive Director; University of Connecticut, Faculty Member

Linda Ross Meyer, Quinnipiac University School of Law, Professor

Brian E. Moran, Malta Justice Initiative, Director; Robinson + Cole LLP, Partner ; The Success Foundation, Inc., Founder

Robert J. O'Hara, Malta Criminal Justice Initiative, Director; United Technologies Corp, Executive; Order of Malta, Member

Edward B. Quinlan, Connecticut Department of Correction, Retired Director of Community Services

Brian Renstrom, Blum Shapiro, Partner

Eric Rey, Beulah Heights Social Integration Program, Executive Director

John S. Santa, Malta Criminal Justice Initiative, Chair; Connecticut State Sentencing Commission, Member; Santa Energy Corporation, Retired Chairman; Order of Malta, Member

Susan O. Storey, State of Connecticut, Chief Public Defender

William L. Tafoya, University of New Haven, Professor and Director of Research for the Henry C. Lee College of Criminal Justice and Forensic Sciences; Federal Bureau of Investigation Special Agent, Retired

Erika M. Tindill, Connecticut Superior Court, Judge; Connecticut Board of Pardons and Paroles, Former Chair

William L. Tuthill, New Opportunities, Inc., Director of Justice and Residential Programs; Connecticut Department of Correction, Retired Warden and Assistant Deputy Commissioner

Scott K. Wilderman, Career Resources, Inc., Executive Director

Nicholas A. Yanicelli, Malta Justice Initiative, President; Susquehanna Enterprises, Partner; Order of Malta, Member

END NOTES

Chapter 1: Executive Summary

i Michelle Alexander, The New Jim Crow: Mass Incarceration in the Age of Colorblindness (New Press 2012) ("Alexander").

ii
Alexander, at 60.

iii
Pew Center on the States, "One in 31 - The Long Reach of American Corrections" (Pew Charitable Trust, 2009).

iv
John Schmitt, Kris Warner and Sarika Gupta, "The High Budgeting Cost of Incarceration," Center for Economic and Policy Research, (Washington, D.C., June 2010) ("Schmitt, Warner and Gupta"). *See* www.cepr.net, at 7.

v
Marc Mauer, *Race to Incarcerate*, rev. ed. (New York: The New Press, 2006), at 33.

vi
Katherine Beckett and Theodore Sasson, *The Politics of Injustice: Crime and Punishment in America* (Thousand Oaks, CA; Sage Publications, 2004), at 163.

vii
Sarah Lawrence and Jeremy Travis, "The New Landscape of Imprisonment: Mapping America's Prison Expansion." The Urban Institute Justice Policy Center, April 2004.

viii
Source: Documentary film "Prison Town, USA" that premiered on PBS on July 25, 2007. See http://www.pbs.org/pov/prisontown/

ix
Schmitt, Warner and Gupta, at 1.

x
Id.

xi
Id.

xii
Id.

xiii
Stemen, Don, "Reconsidering Incarceration: New Directions for Reducing Crime," Vera Institute of Justice (New York, 2007), *available at* http://www.vera.org/download?file=407/veraincarc_vFW2.pdf

xiv
Adam Liptack, "U.S. Prison Population Dwarfs That of Other Nations," New York Times, April 23, 2008, ("Criminologists and legal scholars in other industrialized nations say they are mystified and appalled by the numbers and length of American prison sentences").

xv
The Sentencing Project, Fact Sheet: Trends in U.S. Corrections. *Available at*
http://sentencingproject.org/doc/publications/inc_Trends_in_Corrections_Fact_sheet.pdf

xvi
New York Times Op-Ed, Vanita Gupta, "How to Really End Mass Incarceration," August 14, 2013.

xvii
Michael Tonry, *Thinking About Crime: Sense and Sensibility in America's Penal Culture* (New York: Oxford University Press, 2004) at 20 ("Tonry").

xviii
Alexander, at 7; and Tonry, at 14.

xix
Pew Center on the States, "One in 100: Behind Bars in America," (Washington, D.C., Pew Charitable Trust, 2008), at 5, *available at*
http://www.pewstates.org/uploadedFiles/PCS_Assets/2008/one%20in%20100.pdf

xx
Alexander, at 9; Thomas P. Boncszar, "Prevalence of Imprisonment in the U.S. Population, 1974-2001," U.S. Department of Justice, Bureau of Justice Statistics, August 2003, *available at*
http://www.bjs.gov/content/pub/pdf/piusp01.pdf

Chapter 2: The Explosion of Connecticut's Prison Population

xxi
Nicholas Kristof, Editorial, "Serving Life For This," New York Times, Nov. 13, 2009, http://www.nytimes.com/2013/11/14/opinion/kristof-serving-life-for-this.html?_r=0, (citing Jennifer Turner, American Civil Liberties Union, A Living Death: Life without Parole for Nonviolent Offenses 44 (Vanita Gupta et al. eds., 2013) (an ACLU report that identified 3,200 non-violent offenders sentenced to life in prison)).

xxii
Christopher Reinhart, Office of Legislative Research, Connecticut Prison Population Statistics 1 (2010) *available at* http://www.cga.ct.gov/2010/rpt/2010-R-0030.htm. See also, Office of Policy and Management and Department of Correction: Incarcerated Population 1980 to 2010 (4,147 inmates in July 1980). *Available at* http://www.ct.gov/doc/cwp/view.asp?a=1505&q=265602. The graph of the growth of the prison population in Connecticut in the text is taken from the Office of Policy Management and Department of Correction, *Incarcerated Population 1980-2010, Connecticut Prison Population Statistics available at* http://www.cga.ct.gov/2010/rpt/2010-R-0030.htm, Jan. 15 2010.

xxiii
Criminal Justice Policy & Planning Division, Office of Policy Management, 2014 Annual Forecast of the Prison Population 1 (Office of Policy Management, 2013) *available at*
http://www.ct.gov/opm/lib/opm/cjppd/cjresearch/populationforecast/prison_pop_projection_february_2014_pdf.pdf

xxiv
See The Sentencing Project, "Ending Mass Incarceration: Charting A New Justice Reinvestment," at 2, *available at*
http://sentencingproject.org/doc/publications/sen_Charting%20a%20New%20Justice%20Reinvestment.pdf Connecticut's prison population has fluctuated somewhat of late. As of July 1, 2013, such population stood at 16,988, down from a high of over 19,413 on July 1, 2008. Office of Policy and Management and Department of Correction: Incarcerated Population 1980 to 2010. *Available at* http://www.ct.gov/doc/cwp/view.asp?a=1505&q=265602. Between 2008 and 2012 there was a 3.4 percent decrease. However, there was a population increase in 2013. The population currently remains

below the high mark of 19,000 from January 2008. For February 2014 the population was at 16,839. The projection anticipates a moderate decline through January 2015. Current statistical analysis from the Office of Policy and Management is available at: http://www.ct.gov/opm/lib/opm/cjppd/cjresearch/populationforecast/prison_pop_projection_february_2014_pdf.pdf, 1, 2014]

xxv
Bureau of Justice Statistics: Correctional Populations in the United States Data Service, cited in The Sentencing Project, "Ending Mass Incarceration – Charting A New Justice Reinvestment," at 6. Available at http://sentencingproject.org/doc/publications/sen_Charting%20a%20New%20Justice%20Reinvestment.pdf

xxvi
Mary Lansing and Nancy Dittes, May 1, 2013 Snapshot Data Presentation, presented at the Connecticut Sentencing Commission Meeting (June 20, 2013).

xxvii
Criminal Justice Policy & Planning Division, Office of Policy Management, 2007 Prison Population Projections (Office of Policy Management, 2007) *available at* http://www.ct.gov/opm/LIB/opm/CJPPD/CjResearch/PopulationForecast/PopulationForecastReport2007.pdf

xxviii
Id.

xxix
Id. at 8.

xxx
Id.

xxxi
Justice Policy Institute, "Rethinking the Blues: How We Police in the U.S. and at What Cost," May, 2012 at 4. *Available at:* http://www.justicepolicy.org/uploads/justicepolicy/documents/rethinkingtheblues_final.pdf

xxxii
Id.

xxxiii
James Austin, "Reducing America's Correctional Populations: A Strategic Plan." 12 Justice Research and Policy 9 (2010).

xxxiv
Id.

xxxv
Id.

xxxvi
Id.

xxxvii
**** Olivia Nuzzi, "Prison Reform Is Bigger in Texas", The Daily Beast, April 12, 2014, available at http://www.thedailybeast.com/2014/04/12/prison-reform-is-bigger-in-texas.html

xxxviii
**** *Id.*

xxxix
ᵡᵡᵡᵛⁱⁱ *Id.*

xl
ᵡᵡᵡᵛⁱⁱⁱ *Id.*

xli
ᵡᵡᵡⁱˣ *Id.*

xlii
ˣˡ *Id.*

xliii
ˣˡⁱ *Id.*

xliv
ˣˡⁱⁱ *Id.*

xlv
ˣˡⁱⁱⁱ *Id.*

xlvi

Chapter 3: The Staggering Costs of Mass Incarceration
Nation Inside, *Facts*, Release Aging People in Prison, http://nationinside.org/campaign/release-of-aging-people-in-prison/facts/ (last modified Mar. 23, 2014). Nationwide, prison populations are aging. In 1999, there were 43, 300 prisoners nationwide over the age of 55. In 2011, there were 121,800. Pew Trust Center on the States, *Managing Prison Health Care Spending* (2013) at 9. The aging of Connecticut's prison population will drive its per bed costs significantly higher. The Pew Trust study above found that per-inmate health care spending rose 31 percent from 2001-2008 across 35 states. Connecticut's health-care spending per inmate rose 7 percent over this period, despite a cost-saving partnership with the University of Connecticut's Health Center. Id. at 5, 16. *Available at* http://www.pewstates.org/uploadedFiles/PCS_Assets/2014/PCT_Corrections_Healthcare_Brief_JAN_14.pdf

xlvii
William Bales & Richard Kern, *Introduction from the Guest Editors*, JRP Digest, 2010 at 1 *available at* http://www.jrsainfo.org/pubs/jrp-digest/jrp-digest-vol_12-no_1.pdf

xlviii
Pew Center on the States, *The High Cost of Corrections in America* (2012) *available at* http://www.pewstates.org/research/data-visualizations/the-high-cost-of-corrections-in-america-85899397897

xlix
Legislative Program Review and Investigations Committee, Connecticut General Assembly, *Final Committee Report on Mandatory Minimum Sentences* 29 (2005) *available at* http://www.cga.ct.gov/2005/pridata/Studies/pdf/Minimum_Mandatory_Sentences_Final_Report.PDF

l
General Fund Expenditures Statistics, Department of Correction (Aug. 28, 2013), *available at* http://www.ct.gov/doc/cwp/view.asp?a=1505&q=265586

li
Collectively, the costs borne by taxpayers for state correctional systems is estimated to have risen from $6.7 billion in 1985 to $51 billion in 2010.

National Association of State Budget Officers (NASBO), State Expenditure Report Series 46 (1985-1987) http://www.nasbo.org/sites/default/files/ER_1987.PDF
NASBO, State Expenditure Report Series 6 (2010-2012)
http://www.nasbo.org/sites/default/files/State%20Expenditure%20Report%20%20%28Fiscal%202010-2012%29.pdf
From its general fund and federal contributions, Connecticut spent $83 million on corrections in 1987. NASBO,, State Expenditure Report Series 46 (1985-1987).
http://www.nasbo.org/sites/default/files/ER_1987.PDF
Connecticut spent $647 million on corrections in 2007. NASBO, State Expenditure Report Series 56 (2008). http://www.nasbo.org/sites/default/files/FY08%20State%20Expenditure%20Report.pdf

lii
Office of Fiscal Analysis: Connecticut State Budget FY12 and FY13 Biennium Part 1: Agency Detail, *see* http://www.cga.ct.gov/ofa/Documents/year/BB/2012BB-20110714_FY%2012%20and%20FY%2013%20Connecticut%20Budget%20%20Part%20I.pdf

liii
Vera Institute of Justice, Center On Sentencing and Corrections, The Price of Prisons – What Incarceration Costs Taxpayers: Fact Sheet for State of Connecticut, January 2012 (containing the results of a 40-state survey based on fiscal year 2010 costs). *Available at* http://www.vera.org/sites/default/files/resources/downloads/price-of-prisons-updated-version-021914.pdf

liv
Id. In 2010, Connecticut contributed 80.3 percent of the amount necessary to fully fund pensions in the long run, leaving a shortfall of $36.1 million, plus interest, to provide for corrections employees' pension benefits. *Id.*

lv
Source: 2012 Census of Governments: Employees; See http://www.census.gov

lvi
Department of Correction, "Facilities," *available at* http://www.ct.gov/doc/cwp/view.asp?a=1502&Q=265422]. In 1980, Connecticut had six community correctional centers that housed pretrial offenders and those convicted of misdemeanors. At that time, Connecticut also operated four major correctional institutions: the Cheshire Reformatory for youthful offenders; the Niantic Correctional Institution for female offenders; the Somers Correctional Institution, a maximum security prison; and the Enfield Correctional Institution, a minimum security facility. The expansion of prison facilities was vigorously carried out, particularly during the 1990s. In 1985, Robinson Correctional Institution opened in Enfield, adding 1,462 beds. In 1987, the Osborn Prison Farm was converted to a high-security facility, doubling its size. It was renamed the Enfield Correctional Institution. In 1989, the Bergin Correctional Institution opened in Storrs and expanded in 2001 to 650 beds. In 1990, the Windham City Jail expanded and was renamed the Brooklyn Correctional Center. Also, in 1990, the Willard Correctional Institution was built in Enfield. Cybulski followed in 1993. Those two were consolidated in 1997 and now have 1,071 beds. In 1990-1991, the Hartford Correctional Institution added four new dormitories. In 1993, Cheshire Reformatory expanded to house 1,349 inmates. In 1994, Corrigan Correctional Institution was built in Uncasville. It, along with its neighbor Radgowski, has 1,581 beds. In 1994, York Correctional Institution in Niantic opened. It was consolidated in 1996 with the Niantic Correctional Institution. In 1997, a new housing unit with 196 beds was added. In 1993, MacDougall Correctional Institution opened in Suffield with 975 beds. A comparable facility, Walker, opened in 1992. In 2003, a 600-bed expansion was completed. In 1995, the Northern Correctional Institution in Somers with 227 maximum security inmates was completed. More recently, Connecticut has closed one of its jails and Gates men's facility in Niantic.

lvii
Connecticut Department of Correction 2005 Annual Report, at 5. With Connecticut's investment in new prison facilities, such practice ended in 2004.
http://www.ct.gov/doc/lib/doc/PDF/PDFReport/annualreport2005.pdf

lviii
Compounding the cost burden in Connecticut is the attendant cost of an expanded unionized public work force. The State of Connecticut's corrections budget does not reflect the cost of correctional employee pensions and retiree health plans. According to a 2012 national study by the Vera Institute, "among the participating states, costs outside the corrections department ranged from less than one percent of the total cost of prisons in Arizona to as much as 34 percent in Connecticut." Vera Cost Report, supra note 8.-9.

lix
See http://www.ct.gov/doc/lib/doc/PDF/PDFReport/annualreport2011.pdf

lx
Connecticut Business & Industry Ass'n. (CBIA) Position Paper "Reform Corrections", available at http://www.gov.cbia.com/issues_policies/category/cat/ip-spending (citing to Vera Institute Study).

lxi
Vera Institute of Justice, Center On Sentencing and Corrections, The Price of Prisons – What Incarceration Costs Taxpayers Fact Sheet (January 2012).

lxii
See "Beyond Prison Bars For Better Results, Savings", January 28, 2011, available at http://gov.cbia.com/issues-policies/articles/beyond-prison-bars-for-better-results-savings; see also "Supervision Costs Significantly Less Than Incarceration in Federal System," July 18, 2013, available at http://news.uscourts.gov/supervision-costs-significantly-less-incarceration-federal-system (noting supervision is about one-tenth as expensive as incarceration).

lxiii
Mary Lansing and Nancy Dittes, May 1, 2013 Snapshot Data Presentation, presented to the Connecticut Sentencing Commission on June 20, 2013.

lxiv
Pew Trust Center for States, "Managing Prison Health Care Spending," (2013)

lxv
Handout from Release Aging People In Prison ("RAPP") organization, whose website can be found at http://rappcampaign.com. RAPP's handout estimates the costs of caring for inmates 50 or older ranges from $120,152 to $240,430, as compared with $60,676 annually for prisoners under 50. RAPP also reports that it is projected that by the year 2030, the number of inmates 55 and older will expand by 444 percent as compared with 1980 (440,000 vs. 8,843).

Chapter 4: Recidivism – How is Connecticut Doing ?
lxvi
Kristen Livingstone, "Making the Bad Guy Pay: Growing Use of Cost Shifting as Economic Sanction," reprinted in *Prison Profiteers: Who Makes Money from Mass Incarceration*, edited by Tara Herivel and Paul Wright (New York: The New Press, 2002), at 55.

lxvii
Connecticut General Assembly Office of Program Review and Investigations "Recidivism in Connecticut 2001, Chapter 4, at page 27. *See* http://www.ct.gov/opm/lib/opm/cjppd/cjresearch/recidivismstudy/2001recidivisminConnecticut.pdf .

lxviii
Office of Policy and Management, Recidivism in Connecticut 56 (2001), *Available at* http://www.cga.ct.gov/pri/archives/2001ricrepotchap5.htm

lxix

Id. See also, Pew Center on the States, "State of Recidivism: The Revolving Door of America's Prisons," April 2011, available at
http://www.pewtrusts.org/uploadedfile/www.pewtrusts.org/Reports/Sentencing_and_Corrections/State_Recidivism_Revolving_Door_America_Prison%20.pdf

lxx

Connecticut General Assembly Office of Program Review and Investigations, "Recidivism in Connecticut 2001, Chapter 5, at 56-57, available at
http://www.ct.gov/opm/lib/opm/cjppd/cjresearch/recidivismstudy/2001recidivisminConnecticut.pdf

lxxi

Connecticut Office of Policy and Management, 2011, Recidivism Report, at 5.
http://www.ct.gov/opm/lib/opm/cjppd/cjresearch/recidivismstudy/2011_recidivism_report_final.pdf

lxxii

The Pew Center, "State of Recidivism: The Revolving Door of America's Prisons" (April 2011), at 20, available at
http://www.pewtrusts.org/uploadedFiles/wwwpewtrustsorg/Reports/sentencing_and_corrections/State_Recidivism_Revolving_Door_America_Prisons%20.pdf

lxxiii

See TURNING THE TIDE: FISCAL POLICY CHANGES, BEST PRACTICES AND IDEAS THAT WORK, http://cbia.com/govaff/pdf/2013/TurningTheTide.pdf , pp 16 Citing "State of Recidivism: The Revolving Door of America's Prisons," Pew Center on the States , April 2011, http://www.pewstates.org/uploadedFiles/PCS_Assets/2011/Pew_State_of_Recidivism.pdf

lxxiv

State of Connecticut's Office of Policy and Management's 2011 Annual Recidivism Report, at 6 ("2011 Recidivism Report").

lxxv

See infra, Chapter 13.

lxxvi

Id., at 9.

lxxvii

Id.

lxxviii

Id.

lxxix

Id., at 10.

lxxx

Id.

lxxxi

Criminal Justice Policy and Planning Division, *Incarceration History & Age Analysis* (November 2010), *available at* http://www.ct.gov/opm/lib/opm/cjppd/cjcjpac/incarceration_history_and_age.pdf

lxxxii

Id. at 1.

lxxxiii

Id.

lxxxiv
Id.

lxxxv
Connecticut's Court Support Services Division (CSSD) supervises those on probation. Its Probation Transition and Technical Violations Unit has received national recognition for "best practices" See CSSD's website available at http://www.jud.ct.gov/cssd/adultprob.htm; and Stephen Cox, Kathleen Bantley, Thomas Roscoe, "Evaluation of the Court Support Services Division's Probation Transition Program and Technical Violation Unit; December, 2005, at http://www.jud.ct.gov/external/news/ProbPilot.pdf.

lxxxvi
See P.A. 13-3. *Available at* http://www.ct.gov/doc/cwp/view.asp?a=1502&Q=481866.

lxxxvii
Todd Edwards, "Correctional Good-Time Credits in Southern States", The Council for State Governments (May 2001) available at http://www.slcatlanta.org/publications/HSPS/Goodtime.pdf; and National Conference of State Legislatures, *Cutting Correction Costs: Earned Time Policies for State Prisoners*, (August 2010) available at http://www.ncsl.org/issues-research/justice/earned-time-policies-for-state-prisoners.aspx.

lxxxviii
Id. at 20.

lxxxix
Id. at 21.

xc
Id. at 22-23. The Pew Center on the States, *State of Recidivism: The Revolving Door of America's Prisons* 20 (April 2011).

xci
Yale Criminal Justice Clinic, "Approaches to Reducing Recidivism: Model State Survey," Presented to the Sentencing Policy Committee of the Connecticut Sentencing Commission (May 2013) ("Yale Survey"). Michigan and Missouri were also part of the Bureau of Justice Assistance's (BJA) Justice Reinvestment Initiative (JRI). *Id.*, at 4. The JRI was created by Congress in 2010 to address recidivism. Its focus is on identifying and implementing data-driven approaches that reduce criminal justice spending. States can apply to become part of JRI and receive BJA support. In 2004, Connecticut was the first state to pilot a justice reinvestment program for reducing incarceration for technical probation violations and for "Building Bridges," a program that funds transitional community organizations through the Court Support Services Division. See Sentencing Project, "Ending Mass Incarceration: Charting a New Justice Reinvestment 24" (2012), *available at* http://sentencingproject.org/doc/publications/sen_Charting%20a%20New%20Justice%20Reinvestment.pdf
Connecticut is currently one of the eleven states participating in the JRI program and is working with the Pew Foundation to bring results-first programming to Connecticut. See Justice Center, Council of State Governments, *The National Summit on Justice Reinvestment and Public Safety: Addressing Recidivism, Crime, and Corrections Spending* 55 (2011), *available at* https://www.bja.gov/Publications/CSG_JusticeReinvestmentSummitReport.pdf.

xcii
Yale Survey, at 4.

xciii
Yale Survey, at 5.

xciv
Elizabeth Dwoskin, "Michigan Lets Prisoners Go – And Saves a Bundle," Bloomberg Business Week Magazine, December 1, 2011, available at http://www.businessweek.com/magazine/michigan-lets-

prisoners-goand-saves-a-bundle-12012011.html and Michigan Prisoner Re-Entry Initiative, 2010 Progress Report, at 4 and 15, available at http://www.publicpolicy.com/upload/pdfs/Publications/MPRI_2010_Progress_Report.pdf ("MPRI Progress Report").

xcv
MPRI Progress Report, at 15.

xcvi
Yale Survey, at 8, n. 20.

xcvii
Tamela Aikens, Michigan Prisoner Re-Entry Initiative, available at http://www.dcjp.com/ReEntry.pdf ("Aikens").

xcviii
Yale Survey, at 9. COMPAS (Correction Offender Management Profiling for Alternative Sanctions) is a product offered by Northpoint, Inc. See http://www.northpointinc.com.

xcix
Yale Survey, at 10.

c
Id.

ci
Aikens.

cii
Yale Survey, at 11.

ciii
Id.

civ
Id.

cv
Missouri Working Group on Sentencing and Corrections, "Missouri Working Group on Sentencing and Correction Consensus Report" (December 2011), at 1, available at http://www.senate.mo.gov/12info/comm/special/MWSC-Report.pdf("Missouri Consensus Report").

cvi
Id.

cvii
The Pew Center, "State of Recidivism: The Revolving Door of America's Prisons" (April, 2011), at 23.

cviii
Id.

cix
Yale Survey, at 15.

cx
Missouri Consensus Report, at 4.

cxi
Yale Survey, at 16.

151

cxii
Missouri Reentry Process, Report to the Governor (2011) at 2, available at
http://doc.mo.gov/Documents/mrp/GovReport2011.pdf

cxiii
Id.

cxiv
Yale Survey, at 19.

cxv
Id.

cxvi
Missouri Consensus Report, at 2.

cxvii
Id.

cxviii
The Pew Center, "State of Recidivism: The Revolving Door of America's Prisons" (April, 2011), at 20.

cxix
Id.

cxx
Id.

cxxi
Criminal Justice Commission, "Offender Reentry Programs Preliminary Evaluation (2011), available at
http://www.oregon.gov/CJC/docs/reentry_eval_final.pdf

cxxii
Id.

cxxiii
Oregon Department of Corrections, Community Corrections,
http://www.oregon.gov/Doc/cc/pages/cc_in_oregon.aspx.

cxxiv
Michael Marcus, "Justitia's Bandage: Blind Sentencing, 1 International Journal of Punishment and Sentencing," at 21 25 (2005).

cxxv
Id.

cxxvi
Yale Survey, at 25.
http://www.apainc.org/html/Multnomah%20County%20REC%20Implementation%20Guide.pdf

cxxvii
Id.

cxxviii
Id.

cxxix

The Pew-MacArthur Results First Initiative: "Investing In Programs That Work", The Pew Charitable Trusts and MacArthur Foundation (January 14, 2014) (presented at Building Bridges Revisited Conference at Central Connecticut State University).

cxxx

Id.

cxxxi

For results-based accounting ratings for probation programs, see http://www.jud.ct.gov/statistics/rba.htm; for results-based accounting ratings for prison education programs, see http://www.cga.ct.gov/app/rba/ReportCards/2012Up/Doc_%20Unified%20School%20District%201 _Updated_1_12-12.pdf; for results-based accounting ratings for parole programs, see http://www.cga.ct.gov/app/rba/2011/ReportCards/Department%20of%20Correction_%20Communi ty%20Residential%20Services_%20111510.pdf; and for a general website on RBA results across agencies in Connecticut, see http://www.cga.ct.gov/app/rba/default.asp.
In 2013, the Connecticut Legislature established the Results First Policy Oversight Committee to implement the model with a goal of supporting cost-effective policies and programming in the state. The committee is required to submit annual reports to the governor and General Assembly that recommend measures to implement the Results First model. 2013 Conn Pub Acts 13-247, § 42. http://www.pewstates.org/uploadedFiles/PCS_Assets/2014/RF-State-Successes-brief-ARTFINAL-v5.pdf.

cxxxii

Richard E. Redding, "Juvenile Transfer Laws: An Effective Deterrent To Delinquency," Juvenile Justice Bulletin, Office of Justice Programs, U.S. Department of Justice, June 2010, at 6, available at https://www.ncjrs.gov/pdffiles1/ojjdp/220595.pdf

cxxxiii

Id.

cxxxiv

Dorinda Richetelli et al (Spectrum Associates), "A Second Reassessment of Disproportionate Minority Contact in Connecticut's Juvenile Justice System" (2009), *Available at* http://www.ct.gov/opm/lib/opm/cjppd/cjjjyd/jjydpublications/final_report_dmc_study_may_2009.p df

Chapter 5: The Expanded Length of Prison Terms

cxxxv

Editorial, Nicholas Kristof "Serving Life For This," New York Times, November 13, 2013 (citing "A Living Death," an ACLU Report that identified 3,200 non-violent offenders sentenced for life). *Available at* http://www.nytimes.com/2013/11/14/opinion/kristof-serving-life-for-this.html?_r=0

cxxxvi

"Rethinking Mandatory Sentencing," The Week, September 20, 2013, at 2-3. *Available at* http://theweek.com/article/index/249578/rethinking-mandatory-sentencing .

cxxxvii

Cassia Spohn, *How do Judges Decide?*, "Chapter Six: The Sentencing Reform Movement," at 231. http://www.sagepub.com/upm-data/27009_6.pdf

cxxxviii

Connecticut Legislative Program Review and Investigations Committee, Report: "Factors Impacting Prison Overcrowding" (December 2000), *available at* http://www.ct.gov/opm/lib/opm/cjppd/cjresearch/recidivismstudy/whatiscausingprisonovercrowdin g.pdf ("Prison Overcrowding Report")

cxxxix
Connecticut Legislative Program Review and Investigations Committee, Report: "Briefing on Mandatory Minimums" (2005), available at http://www.cga.ct.gov/2005/pridata/Studies/Mandatory_Minimum_Senteces_Briefing.htm ("Mandatory Minimums Briefing"), at 26. See also, Central Connecticut State University, Timeline of Major Criminal Justice Policies and Other Initiatives, prepared for 2006 Conference on Building Bridges II: An Evaluation of Connecticut's Justice Reinvestment Initiative, *available at* https://www.ccsu.edu/uploaded/websites/IMRP/For_Building_Bridges_II_Page/Final_Timeline_of_criminal_justice_policies.pdf

cxl
Mandatory Minimums Briefing at 26.

cxli
Id. at 26. Connecticut Office of Legal Research, Report 2012-R-0241, Emilee Mooney Scott, "Crimes With Mandatory Minimum Prison Sentences," February 16, 2011, available at http://www.cga.ct.gov/2010/rpt/2010-r-0241.htm ("OLR Mandatory Minimums Report").

cxlii
Mandatory Minimums Briefing; Mandatory Minimums Report.

cxliii
Mandatory Minimums Briefing.

cxliv
Id. at 26

cxlv
Id. at 26

cxlvi
Id. at 26

cxlvii
Id.

cxlviii
Id.

cxlix
Id.

cl
Id.

cli
Id.

clii
Id.

cliii
Id.

cliv
Id.

clv
Bureau of Justice Assistance, Final Report to Congress: "Violent Offenders and Truth-In-Sentencing Formula Grant Program" (February 2012) U.S. Department of Justice, at 9-10. *Available at* https://www.bja.gov/Publications/VOITIS-Final-Report.pdf

clvi
Id.

clvii
Id.

clviii
Id.

clix
Quinnipiac Legal Clinic, Yale Lowenstein International Rights Clinic, "Youth Matters," (March 2013) http://www.cga.ct.gov/2014/JUDdata/Tmy/2014HB-05221-R000303-Youth%20Matters%20Report%20by%20Quinnipiac%20Un.%20School%20of%20Law%20and%20Yale%20Law%20School%20Allard%20K.%20Lowenstein%20International%20Human%20Right%20Clinic-TMY.PDF

clx
Id.

clxi
Mandatory Minimums Briefing, supra.

clxii
Corrections Statistics By State, National Institute of Corrections. *See* http://nicic.gov/statestats/?st=CT.

clxiii
Mandatory Minimums Briefing, supra.

clxiv
Prison Overcrowding Report, supra.

clxv
Mandatory Minimums Briefing, supra.

clxvi
Mandatory Minimums Briefing, supra.

clxvii
Jim Dwyer, "Fewer Lockups, Drop in Crime During Bloomberg Tenure," New York Post, December 27, 2013, at 4, Col. 3.

clxviii
New York Times Editorial, "Rewriting City's Record on Prisons," January 3, 2014, A14, at 1. *Available at* http://www.nytimes.com/2014/01/03/nyregion/rewriting-the-citys-record-on-prisons.html?_r=0

clxix
Id.

clxx
Justice Research and Policy, JRP Digest, Vol. 12, No. 1, 2010 "Summary of Articles – Special Issue On Sentencing and Corrections in the States," at 6. ("JRP Summary"). *Available at*: http://www.jrsa.org/pubs/jrp-digest/jrp-digest-articles/jrp-digest-article-0084.htm

clxxi
Id.

clxxii
Id.

clxxiii
Id.

clxxiv
Id.

clxxv
Id.

clxxvi
Id.

clxxvii
Useem, B., "Right-Sizing Corrections in New York," Justice Research and Policy, Vol. 12, No. 1, 2010, 89-112.

clxxviii
Id.

clxxix
Id.

clxxx
Id.

clxxxi
Id. The 30-day program was known as the Edgecombe Technical Violation Program and the 90-day program was known as the Willard Drug Treatment Campus.

clxxxii
Id.

clxxxiii
Id.

clxxxiv
Pew Center on the States, *State of Recidivism: The Revolving Door of America's Prisons* (April 2011) *Available at* http://www.pewtrusts.org/uploadedFiles/wwwpewtrustsorg/Reports/sentencing_and_corrections/Sta te_Recidivism_Revolving_Door_America_Prisons%20.pdf (cited by CBIA Position Paper: "Reform Corrections," January 23, 2013. *Available at* http://gov.cbia.com/issues_policies/article/reform-corrections

clxxxv
Id.

clxxxvi
Id.

Chapter 6: Crime Rates In Connecticut – Are We Safer ?

clxxxvii
National Center for Policy Analysis, "Crime and Punishment in America," by Morgan O. Reynolds at 2. *Available at* http://www.ncpa.org/pdfs/st193.pdf

clxxxviii
Connecticut Criminal Justice Policy and Planning Division's Comparative Analysis of Crime Rates:
Connecticut, the United States and Adjacent Northeast States – 1960-2007, *available at*
http://www.ct.gov/opm/lib/opm/cjppd/cjresearch/projects/crimestatistcs/20080923_crimeinus2007
_final.pdf

clxxxix
.Id.

cxc
Id.

cxci
JRP Digest: "A Summary of Articles from Justice Research and Policy," Vol. 12, No. 1 (2010); Special
Issue on Sentencing and Corrections In the States, at 2.

cxcii
Id. at 35.

cxciii
Id. at 36.

cxciv
See Justice Policy Institute Report, "Disparity by Design: How Drug Free Zone Laws Impact Racial
Disparity and Fail to Protect Youth," (March 2008) *available at*
http://www.drugpolicy.org/docUploads/SchoolZonesReport06.pdf

cxcv
"Connecticut Criminal Justice and Planning Division's Ranking of 50 States by Selected Crime Rates:
2005 to 2007," at 1, *available at*
http://www.ct.gov/opm/lib/opm/cjppd/cjresearch/projects/crimestatistcs/20080923_50staterankings
_final.pdf

cxcvi
Corrections Statistics by State, National Institute of Corrections. *Available at*
http://nicic.gov/statestats/?st=CT

cxcvii
Federal Bureau of Investigation, Crime in the U.S. 2012, Tables 1 and 5. *Available at*
http://www.fbi.gov/about-us/cjis/ucr/crime-in-the-u.s/2012/crime-in-the-u.s.-2012/resource-
pages/about-cius/about-cius

cxcviii
See "Reflecting on Connecticut's Pioneering Justice Reinvestment Work," by Michael Thompson,
Director, Council of State Governments Justice Center, presented at January 14, 2014, Building Bridges
Revisited Seminar at Central Connecticut State University.

cxcix
Connecticut Criminal Justice Policy and Planning Division's Comparative Analysis of Crime Rates:
Connecticut, the United States and Adjacent Northeast States – 1960-2007, at 1 *available at*
www.ct.gov/opm/criminaljustice/research.

cc
Remarks of Patrick Hynes, Ph.D. at Building Bridges Revisited Seminar held at Central Connecticut
State University on January 14, 2014, at 3.

cci
"FBI Stats – Crime Declines," Stamford Advocate, March 5, 2014, at A-1, Col. 1.

ccii
Id.

Chapter 7: Who Resides in Connecticut's Prisons?

cciii
Judiciary Committee Hearing Transcript for 3/23/2012: Hearing on H.B. 5546 Before the Conn. Judiciary Comm., 2012 Leg., Sess. (Conn. 2012) (testimony of Wally Lamb).

cciv
Available at Correctional Law Enforcement Agency Case Reports 1980-2010.

ccv
State of Connecticut Department of Emergency Services and Public Protection, Crimes Analysis Unit, "Annual Report of the Uniform Crime Reporting Program: Crime in Connecticut," 11-15 (2012)("C in C 2012"); *available at* http://www.dpsdata.ct.gov/dps/ucr/data/2012/Crime%20In%20Connecticut%20COMPLETE%202012.pdf; Office of Policy and Management, "Prison Population Forecast 2012," *available at* http://www.ct.gov/opm/lib/opm/cjppd/cjresearch/populationforecast/2012_prison_population_forecast_final.pdf (includes prison population data from 1985 to 2008).

ccvi
E. Ann Carson & Daniela Golinelli, Bureau of Justice Statistics, United States Department of Justice, Prisoners in 2012 – Advance Counts 10, (2013).

ccvii
Christopher Reinhart, "People Incarcerated for Non-Violent Crimes," 2010-R-0157 (Connecticut Office of Legislative Research, March 17, 2010) *available at* http://www.cga.ct.gov/2010/rpt/2010-R-0157.htm. This OLR report estimated that in 2010, 63 percent of those in prison in Connecticut had committed a non-violent offense. DOC representatives interviewed for this report estimated that over half of those in prison committed violent crimes.

ccviii
Department of Correction, Annual Report 1 (2012), *available at* http://www.ct.gov/doc/lib/doc/PDF/PDFReport/annualreport2012.pdf.

ccix
Mary Lansing and Nancy Dittes, May 1, 2013, Snapshot Data Presentation, presented to the Connecticut Sentencing Commission on June 20, 2013.

ccx
The Sentencing Project, "Facts about Prisons and People in Prison" 2 (2014) *available at* http://www.sentencingproject.org/doc/publications/inc_Facts%20About%20Prisons.pdf; The Sentencing Project, Trends in U.S. Corrections Fact Sheet (2012), *available at* http://sentencingproject.org/doc/publications/inc_Trends_in_Corrections_Fact_sheet.pdf.

ccxi
E. Ann Carson and William J. Sabol, Bureau of Justice Statistics, United States Department of Justice, Prisoners in 2011 10 (2012) *available at* http://www.bjs.gov/content/pub/pdf/p11.pdf.

ccxii
E. Ann Carson and William J. Sabol, Bureau of Justice Statistics, United States Department of Justice, Prisoners in 2011 10 (2012) *available at* http://www.bjs.gov/content/pub/pdf/p11.pdf.

ccxiii
Mary Lansing and Nancy Dittes, *supra* note 7.

ccxiv
E. Ann Carson & Daniela Golinelli, Bureau of Justice Statistics, United States Department of Justice, Prisoners in 2012, Trends in Admissions and Releases, 1991-2011 (December 2013) *available at* http://www.bjs.gov/content/pub/pdf/p12tar9112.pdf ; The Sentencing Project, Federal Prison Fact Sheet (2011), *available at* http://www.sentencingproject.org/doc/publications/inc_FederalPrisonFactsheet_March2011.pdf; The Sentencing Project, "Trends in U.S. Corrections Fact Sheet" (2012), *available at* http://sentencingproject.org/doc/publications/inc_Trends_in_Corrections_Fact_sheet.pdf.

ccxv
The Sentencing Project, "Trends in U.S. Corrections Fact Sheet" (2012), *available at* http://sentencingproject.org/doc/publications/inc_Trends_in_Corrections_Fact_sheet.pdf.

ccxvi
Id.

ccxvii
Mike Krause, Independence Institute, The Case for Further Sentencing Reform in Colorado 3 (2011), *available at* http://liberty.i2i.org/files/2011/01/IP_1_2011_a.pdf.

ccxviii
Eric Lotke and Jason Ziedenberg, Justice Policy Institute, Tipping Point: Maryland's Overuse of Incarceration and the Impact on Community Safety 2 (2005).

ccxix
Bureau of the Census, Quick Facts (2013), *available at* http://quickfacts.census.gov/qfd/states/00000.html.

ccxx
The Sentencing Project, Fact Sheet: Trends in U.S. Corrections (2012), *available at* http://sentencingproject.org/doc/publications/inc_Trends_in_Corrections_Fact_sheet.pdf.

ccxxi
Id.

ccxxii
Mary Lansing and Nancy Dittes, *supra* note 7.

ccxxiii
Connecticut Juvenile Justice Alliance, Fact Sheet: Race and Juvenile Justice, *available at* http://www.ctjja.org/colorofjustice/toolkit/Factsheet-raceandjj.pdf *See also* Dorinda M. Richetelli et al., (Spectrum Associates), "A Second Reassessment of Disproportionate Minority Contact in Connecticut's Juvenile Justice System" (2009), *available at* http://www.ct.gov/opm/lib/opm/cjppd/cjjjyd/jjydpublications/final_report_dmc_study_may_2009.pdf; Office of Policy and Management, "Biennial Report on Disproportionate Minority Contact" (December 31, 2011), *available at* http://www.ct.gov/opm/lib/opm/cjppd/cjjjyd/juststart/DMCBiennialReport123111.pdf. The disparate impact of Connecticut's war on drugs on minorities is mirrored by federal statistics for the District of Connecticut. Blacks and Hispanics constituted 84.2 percent of federal drug offenders in 2012. U.S. Sentencing Commission, Interactive Sourcebook (2012) *available at* http://isb.ussc.gov. Most federal drug offenders in Connecticut from 2009-2012 were Black or Hispanic, male and under 36 years of age. *Id.* From 2006-2012, of the total number of federal drug trafficking offenders in Connecticut, 87.9 percent did not attend college and 41.9 percent did not finish high school. *Id.*

ccxxiv
Department of Correction, Annual Report 6 (2012), *available at* http://www.ct.gov/doc/lib/doc/PDF/PDFReport/annualreport2012.pdf.

ccxxv
Connecticut Juvenile Justice Alliance, Fact Sheet: Race and Juvenile Justice, *available at* http://www.ctjja.org/colorofjustice/toolkit/Factsheet-raceandji.pdf *See also* Dorinda M. Richetelli et al., (Spectrum Associates), "A Second Reassessment of Disproportionate Minority Contact in Connecticut's Juvenile Justice System" (2009), *available at* http://www.ct.gov/opm/lib/opm/cjppd/cjjjyd/jjydpublications/final_report_dmc_study_may_2009.pdf; Office of Policy and Management, "Biennial Report on Disproportionate Minority Contact" (December 31, 2011), *available at* http://www.ct.gov/opm/lib/opm/cjppd/cjjjyd/juststart/DMCBiennialReport123111.pdf.

ccxxvi
The Sentencing Project, Facts about Prisons and People in Prison 2 (2014), *available at* http://www.sentencingproject.org/doc/publications/inc_Facts%20About%20Prisons.pdf.

ccxxvii
Id.

ccxxviii
Mary Lansing and Nancy Dittes, *supra* note 6.

ccxxix
Dr. Stephanie Covington, *Women and the Criminal Justice System*, 17 Women's Health Issues 180 (2007) (citing B. Bloom et al., "Gender-Responsive Strategies: Research Practice and Guiding Principles For Women Offenders," (U.S. Department of Justice, National Institute of Corrections 2003)).

ccxxx
Id. at 181 (citing Doris J. James and Lauren E. Glaze, "Mental Health Problems of Prisoners and Jail Inmates," (Bureau of Justice Statistics, Washington, D.C. 2006)).

ccxxxi
Barbara E. Bloom and Stephanie S. Covington, "Addressing the Mental Health Needs of Women Offenders," in Mental Health Issues Across The Criminal Justice System 161 Women's Mental Health Issues Across the Criminal Justice System 161 (Rosemary Gido and Lanette Dalley eds., 2008) (citing Linda A. Teplin, et al., "Prevalence of Psychiatric Disorders Among Incarcerated Women; I. Pretrial Jail Detainees," 53 Arch Gen Psychiatry 505 (1996) and B. Kathleen Jordan et al., "Prevalence of Psychiatric Disorders Among Incarcerated Women: II Convicted Felons Entering Prison," 53 Arch Gen Psychiatry 1048 (1996).

ccxxxii
Id. at 170 (citing Doris J. James and Lauren E. Glaze, "Mental Health Problems of Prisoners and Jail Inmates, " (Bureau of Justice Statistics, Washington, D.C. 2006)).

ccxxxiii
Id. at 162,(citing Doris J. James and Lauren E. Glaze, "Mental Health Problems of Prisoners and Jail Inmates," (Bureau of Justice Statistics, Washington, D.C. 2006)).

ccxxxiv
Covington, *supra* note 27 at 181 (citing Bonnie L. Green et al., "Trauma Exposure, Mental Health Functioning, and Program Needs of Women in Jail," 51 Crime and Delinquency 133, 141 (2005).

ccxxxv
Bloom, *supra* note 29, at 162 (citing Doris J. James and Lauren E. Glaze, "Mental Health Problems of Prisoners and Jail Inmates," (Bureau of Justice Statistics, Washington, D.C. 2006)).

ccxxxvi
Covington, *supra* note 27 at 181.

ccxxxvii
Bloom, *supra* note 27 at 167-174.

ccxxxviii
Id.

Chapter 8: Inside Connecticut's Prisons – What's Going On ?

ccxxxix
D'Amora, David, Larke Huang, Fred Osher, Anita Pollard, and Ruby Qazilbash. "Adults with Behavioral Health Needs Under Correctional Supervision: A Shared Framework for Reducing Recidivism and Promoting Recovery." Webinar held by the Council of State Governments Justice Center, New York, NY, October 2, 2012.

ccxl
Id.

ccxli
CBS News *60 Minutes* Story, "Nowhere To Go--Mentally Ill Youth In Crisis", first aired February 3, 2014: see www.cbsnews.com/news/mentally-ill-youth-in-crisis.

ccxlii
Huang, at 4.

ccxliii
"Judge Extends Mandate To Aid Mentally Ill City Inmates," *New York Law Journal*, April 22, 2014, available at http://www.newyorklawjournal.com/id=1202651976082?kw=judge%20Extends%20City.

ccxliv
Id.

ccxlv
Prison Release Statistics, October 29, 2013. OLR Research Report 2013-R-0413, available at http://www.cga.ct.gov/2013/rpt/2013-R-0413.htm

ccxlvi
Id.

ccxlvii
This is a composite profile of an offender for illustrative purposes.

ccxlviii
See generally, John J. Dilulio, "Governing Prisons: A Comparative Study of Correctional Management," 94 Am. J. Sociology 902 (1989)(discussing general prison management, including the attitudinal factors displayed by correctional staff on this subject).

ccxlix
See, Conn. Dept. of Corrections, Directive No. 9.4, Restrictive Status (2010) *available at* http://www.ct.gov/doc/LIB/doc/PDF/AD/ad0904.pdf.

ccl
James Warren, Editorial, *A Devastating Game of Solitaire*, N.Y. Daily News, March 2, 2014, at 39.

ccli
Id.

cclii
Id.

ccliii
Id.

ccliv
For a compact review of the deterrence principle and related research, *see*, Valerie Wright, "Deterrence in Criminal Justice: Evaluating Certainty vs. Severity of Punishment" (2010) *available at* http://www.sentencingproject.org/doc/Deterrence%20Briefing%20.pdf.

cclv
In Connecticut, the DOC was formed in 1968 as an amalgamation of the State Jail Administration and the four heretofore independent institutions: The Connecticut Reformatory (Cheshire), the Connecticut State Prison and Prison Farm (Somers-Osborn), and the Connecticut Farm for Women (Niantic). "History of the Connecticut Department of Correction," Department of Correction, http://www.ct.gov/doc/cwp/view.asp?a=1500&q=378460 (last modified Aug. 3, 2010).

cclvi
Compare with, Ram Subramanian and Alison Shames, "Sentencing and Prison Practices in Germany and the Netherlands: Implications for the United States" (2013) *available at* http://www.vera.org/sites/default/files/resources/downloads/european-american-prison-report-v3.pdf (exploring the confinement and rehabilitation priorities in Germany and the Netherlands as contrasted with practices in the U.S.).

cclvii
This is a composite sketch of an offender utilized for illustrative purposes.

cclviii
This is a composite sketch of an offender utilized for illustrative purposes.

cclix
This is a real life case drawn from an article appearing in the New Haven Register on August 27, 2003.

cclx
See, Department of Correction, 2012 Annual Report 27 & 32 (2012), *available at* http://www.ct.gov/doc/lib/doc/PDF/PDFReport/annualreport2012.pdf. Conn. Dept. of Correction, Directive No. 9.7, Offender Management (2007), available at http://www.ct.gov/doc/LIB/doc/PDF/AD/ad0907.pdf.

cclxi
See, Conn. Dept. of Correction, Directive No. 4.2A, Risk Reduction Earned Credit (2013), *available at* http://www.ct.gov/doc/lib/doc/PDF/AD/ad0402a.pdf.

cclxii
According to the Department of Correction, the current average cost per inmate per day is $95.16 and the cost of supervising an offender in the community is $32.66 per day. Department of Correction FAQ, *available at* http://www.ct.gov/doc/cwp/view.asp?q=265472. A Connecticut legislative oversight committee reported in 2000 that maximum security facilities cost almost $122 per day, while minimum security facilities, which provided the most programming and treatment, cost only $53 per day. Connecticut Legislative Program Review and Investigations Committee, *Report on Prison Overcrowding*, Chapter 2 (December 2000), *available at* http://www.ct.gov/opm/lib/opm/cjppd/cjresearch/recidivismstudy/whatiscausingprisonovercrowding.pdf.

cclxiii
See, Conn. Dept. of Correction, Directive No. 9.2, Offender Classification (2006) *available at* http://www.ct.gov/doc/LIB/doc/PDF/AD/ad0902.pdf.

cclxiv
See, Conn. Department of Correction, Compendium of Programs and Services for Offender Population, (2013), *available at* http://www.ct.gov/doc/lib/doc/PDF/Compendium/CompendiumALL.pdf (describes specific program options available to inmates and the facilities where such services are provided).

cclxv
All institutional educational services are provided by Unified School District #1, which is operated by
the DOC for DOC inmates exclusively. *See*, Conn. Dept. of Corrections, Directive No. 10.2, Inmate
Education (2009) *available at* http://www.ct.gov/doc/LIB/doc/PDF/AD/ad1002.pdf. There are a
range of vocational education courses covering auto repair, graphic arts, culinary arts, commercial
cleaning and a few other skills. Unified School District #1, Conn. Department of Corrections, 2011-
2012 Annual Performance Report 10-15 *available at*
http://www.ct.gov/doc/lib/doc/PDF/PDFReport/EducationStatistics1112.pdf. College-level courses
are available at certain institutions through cooperative arrangements. *Id.* No one institution offers the
entire range of services. The GED is the most common educational program offered for institutions.
According to DOC's 2012 Annual Report, 76 percent of inmates lack a GED or high school diplomas.
Department of Corrections, *supra* note 4 at 1. During 2010-2011, 16,905 students enrolled in school.
Only 574 were awarded GEDs. *Id.* at 27.

cclxvi
Conn. Dept. of Correction, Directive No. 6.3, Population Counts (5) (A) (1) (2007) *available at*
http://www.ct.gov/doc/LIB/doc/PDF/AD/ad0603.pdf.

cclxvii
Bureau of Justice Assistance, U.S. Dep't of Justice, Report to Congress: "Violent Offender Incarceration
and Truth In Sentencing Incentive Formula Grant Program" (2012), *available at*
https://www.bja.gov/Publications/VOITIS-Final-Report.pdf.

cclxviii
See, Ellis Cose, "The Dawn of a New Movement," Newsweek, April 23, 2006,
http://www.newsweek.com/dawn-new-movement-107875.

cclxix
Department of Correction, *supra* note 4 at 1.

cclxx
Id.

cclxxi
Id. at 28. See also, Connecticut Unified School District #1, Annual Report 3, 15 (2011-2012), *available at*
http://www.ct.gov/doc/lib/doc/PDF/PDFReport/EducationStatistics1112.pdf. 574 GEDs awarded,
20 regular high school diplomas awarded, students gained an average of 2 years, 2 months in reading, 2
years 3 months in math, and 8 months in language arts, 256 completed college courses (through
programming provided gratis by local colleges or through correspondence courses paid for by inmates
or through federal grants for a few youth offenders who met particular federal requirements), 2,602
students attended educational or vocation programs, 392 received certificates of vocational completion,
191 received Connecticut Career Certificates, 804 received certificates of completion for participation in
re-entry classes.

cclxxii
Education Services, Department of Correction, http://www.ct.gov/doc/cwp/view.asp?q=265554 (last
modified Jan. 2, 2014).

cclxxiii
See, Daniel A. Passarell, "The Effect Earning a GED While Incarcerated Has On Recidivism Rates: A
Research Synthesis," (May 2013)(MSEd thesis, The College at Brockport: State University of New York),
available at http://digitalcommons.brockport.edu/ehd_theses/181/); see also, Lois M. Davis et al.,
"Evaluating the Effectiveness of Correctional Education: A Meta Analysis of Programs That Provide
Education to Incarcerated Adults" (2013) *available at*
http://www.rand.org/pubs/research_reports/RR266.html.

cclxxiv
Editorial,"Gov. Cuomo Drops the Ball," New York Times, April 9, 2014, at A22.

cclxxv
State of Connecticut Sentencing Commission, 2012 Annual Report 7-9 (2012) *available at* http://www.ct.gov/opm/lib/opm/cjppd/cjabout/sentencingcommission/2012_sentencing_commissio n_annual_report.pdf.

cclxxvi
Id. at 7.

cclxxvii
Id. at 7.

cclxxviii
Id. at 7-9.

cclxxix
Id.

cclxxx
Linda Chavez, Editorial, "The Federal War On School Discipline," New York Post, Jan. 11, 2014, at 19.

cclxxxi
The Economic Mobility Project and The Public Safety Performance Project, The Pew Charitable Trusts, Collateral Costs: Incarceration's Effect on Economic Mobility 9 (2010), *available at* http://www.pewtrusts.org/uploadedFiles/wwwpewtrustsorg/Reports/Economic_Mobility/Collateral% 20Costs%20FINAL.pdf.

cclxxxii
 "Lessons from European Prisons,"New York Times, Nov. 7, 2012, at A34.

cclxxxiii
Id.

cclxxxiv
Id.

Chapter 9: Punishment Beyond Incarceration – Life on the Outside
cclxxxv
Maurice's story is a fictional composite drawn for illustrative purposes from "Chapter Four: The Cruel Hand" in Michelle Alexander's *The New Jim Crow: Mass Incarceration in the Age of Colorblindness* 142-43 (New York: The New Press, 2012) citing the American Bar Association's Task Force on Collateral Sanctions, Introduction, Proposed Standards vs. Collateral Sanctions and Administrative Disqualification of Convicted Persons, draft, January 18, 2002. In 2002, the U.S. Supreme Court held that public housing tenants can be evicted regardless of whether they had personal knowledge of or participated in the criminal activity upon which the conviction was based. *See Department of Housing and Urban Development vs. Rucker*, 535 U.S. 125 (2002).

cclxxxvi
Connecticut Office of Policy and Management, 2011 Recidivism Report (February 11, 2011). Available at: http://www.ct.gov/opm/lib/opm/cjppd/cjresearch/recidivismstudy/2011_recidivism_report_final.pdf

cclxxxvii
Connecticut Department of Correction, "Annual Performance Report 2011-2012" (2012). Available at: http://www.ct.gov/doc/lib/doc/PDF/PDFReport/EducationStatistics1112.pdf.

cclxxxviii
Wesleyan, Trinity and Quinnipiac all participate in programs that educate prisoners. Wesleyan has been a pioneer in creating a multi-year prison education project at two prison facilities in Connecticut. *See* Center for Prison Education, Wesleyan University. http://www.wesleyan.edu/cpe.

cclxxxix
U.S .Department of Justice Office Of Public Affairs, Justice and Education Departments Announce New Research Showing Prison Education Reduces Recidivism, Saves Money, Improves Employment, (August 22, 2013) *available at* http://www.justice.gov/opa/pr/2013/August/13-ag-948.html.

ccxc
Jeremy Travis, Amy Solomon, and Michelle Waul, "From Prison to Home: The Dimensions and Consequences of Prisoner Re-entry" (Washington, D.C.: Urban Institute, 2001).

ccxci
Bruce Western, *Punishment and Inequality in America* 90 (New York: Russell Sage Foundation, 2006).

ccxcii
Id., at 91.

ccxciii
Jeremy Travis, "But They All Come Back: Rethinking Prisoner Reentry," Sentencing and Corrections: Issues for the 21st Century. U.S. Department of Justice Office of Justice Programs (May 2000). *Available at* https://www.ncjrs.gov/txtfiles1/nij/181413.txt.

ccxciv
Connecticut Office of Policy and Management and Connecticut Statistical Analysis Center at CCSU, Recidivism Study, Annual Report (2007). *Available at:* http://www.ct.gov/opm/LIB/opm/cjppd/cjabout/rptcompplan/RptCompPlan03072007.pdf (Appendix G).

ccxcv
Timothy Hughes and Doris James Wilson, "Reentry Trends in the United States." U.S. Dept. of Justice Office of Justice Programs Bureau of Justice Statistics (August 20, 2003). *Available at* http://www.bjs.gov/content/pub/pdf/reentry.pdf.

ccxcvi
Alexander, at 142.

ccxcvii
Edward Rhine, William Smith and Ronald Jackson, *Paroling Authorities: Recent History and Current Practices* (Laurel, Maryland: American Correctional Association, 1991).

ccxcviii
Legal Action Center, "After Prison: Roadblocks to Re-entry, a Report on State Legal Barriers Facing People with Criminal Records," 10 (New York: Legal Action Center, 2004), *available at* http://www.lac.org/roadblocks-to-reentry/upload/lacreport/LAC_PrintReport.pdf.

ccxcix
William Kaempffer, "Alderman Vote To 'Ban The Box," New Haven Register, February 19, 2009, http://www.nhregister.com/general-news/20090218/aldermen-vote-to-ban-the-box ; P.A. 10-42, Susan Price, Sr. Attorney, "Ban the Box Laws,",Office of Legislative Research, July 22, 2010, 2010-R-0294, http://www.cga.ct.gov/2010/rpt/2010-R-0294.htm.

ccc
Alexander, at 154-155.

ccci
See "Note: Stymied By the Stigma Of A Criminal Conviction: Connecticut and the Struggle to Relieve Collateral Consequences," 31 Quinnipiac Law Review 985 (2013).

cccii
Alexander, at 155.

cccciii
Rachel L. McLean and Michelle D. Thompson, "Repaying Debts" (New York: Council of State Governments Justice Center, 2007), cited in Alexander at 155.

cccciv
Dennis Culhane, et al., the "New York/New York Agreement Cost Study: The Impact of Supportive Housing on Services Use for Homeless Mentally Ill Individuals" (New York; Corporation for Supporting Housing, 2001), at 4.

ccccv
Alexander at 157, citing Legal Action Center, "Opting Out of Federal Ban on Food Stamps and TANF; Summary of State Laws"; www.lac.org/tooklits/TANF/TANF.htm.

ccccvi
Alexander, at 157.

ccccvii
Legal Action Center, "Opting Out of Federal Ban on Food Stamps and TANF; Summary of State Laws"; www.lac.org/tooklits/TANF/TANF.htm.

ccccviii
Alexander, at 158.

ccccix
Pew Center on the States, "Collateral Costs: Incarceration's Effect on Economic Mobility," Pew Foundation (2010) *available at* http://www.pewstates.org/research/reports/collateral-costs-85899373309?p=1.

ccccx
Id. at 5. It is estimated that incarceration costs adult offenders aged 45 at least $15,000 per year after release from prison (based on 2009 data). Ex-offenders made on average $14.57/hour vs. $16.33/hour for non-offenders; ex-offenders worked 39 weeks/year vs. 48 weeks/year for non-offenders; and ex-offenders made $23,500/year vs. $39,100/year for non-offenders. *Id.* It is 5-6 times less likely for an ex-offender to experience upward mobility. *Id.*

ccccxi
"Throw The Book At Them -- Hudson Link Offers New York Prisoners A Way Forward Through College – Level Education," New York Post, Higher Education Section, April 2, 2014, at 45.

ccccxii
Id. The Hudson Link program is also the subject of a recent HBO documentary entitled, "The University of Sing Sing."

ccccxiii
Connecticut Sentencing Commission, Annual Report 8-10 (2012), *available at* http://www.ct.gov/opm/lib/opm/cjppd/cjabout/sentencingcommission/2012_sentencing_commission_annual_report.pdf See also, Connecticut Sentencing Commission Recidivism Reduction Committee, "Draft Report: Evidence-Based Reentry Initiatives Devoted to Strengthening Positive Social Relationships," *Available at:* http://www.ct.gov/opm/lib/opm/cjppd/cjabout/sentencingcommission/20120920_recidivism_reduction_strengthening_positive_social_relationships.pdf.

Chapter 10: Avoiding Incarceration/No-Entry Diversion Programs

ccccxiv
~~ccxcii~~ These three cases are composites for illustrative purposes.

cccxv
Patrick Coleman, Jeffrey Felten-Green, Geroma Oliver, BJA, "Practitioner Perspectives, Connecticut's Alternative Sanctions Program," U.S. Department of Justice, Bureau of Justice Programs, Bureau of Justice Assistance (October 1998), *available at* https://www.ncjrs.gov/pdffiles/172870.pdf.

cccxvi
Connecticut Office of Legislative Research, "Diversionary Programs for Offenders with Psychiatric Disorders," 2008-R-0386 (June 27, 2008). See also, Russ Immarigeon and Judith Greene, Diversion Works, "How Connecticut Can Downsize Prisons, Improve Public Safety and Save Money with a Comprehensive Mental Health and Substance Abuse Approach," A Better Way Foundation Report Justice Strategies (April 2008) (commissioned by the Drug Policy Alliance), *available at* http://www.drugpolicy.org/docUploads/DiversionWorks.pdf.

cccxvii
Id.

cccxviii
J. McGregor Smyth, Jr., "From Arrest to Reintegration: A Model For Mitigating Collateral Consequences of Criminal Proceedings," American Bar Association, Criminal Justice, 24 Crim. Just. 42 (Fall 2009), *available at* http://www.americanbar.org/content/dam/aba/publishing/criminal_justice_section_newsletter/crimjust_cjmag_24_3_smyth.authcheckdam.pdf.

cccxix
Data compiled by Ivan Kuzyk, State of Connecticut, Office of Policy and Management, Criminal Justice Division.

cccxx
Families in Crisis, Inc., Hartford, Connecticut. http://www.familiesincrisis.org.

cccxxi
Attorney Nadine Nevins, Connecticut Legal Services, Inc., "The Collateral Consequences of a Criminal Conviction: Employment," Public Defender Services Training (October, 2013), *materials available at* http://ctpublicdefendertraining.com/materials.htm.

cccxxii
Attorney Elizabeth Pisarski-Buchholz, Statewide Legal Services of Connecticut, *The Collateral Consequences of Arrest, Incarceration and Conviction on Public Benefits*, Public Defender Services Training (October, 2013), *materials available at* http://ctpublicdefendertraining.com/materials.htm.

cccxxiii
Attorney Allison M. Near, New Haven Legal Assistance Assoc., *Collateral Consequences of Criminal Proceedings on Subsidized Housing*, Public Defender Services Training (October, 2013), *materials available at* http://ctpublicdefendertraining.com/materials.htm.

cccxxiv
Attorney Robert E. Henry, Esq., *Collateral Consequences of Conviction for Military Service Members*, Public Defender Services Training (October, 2013), *materials available at* http://ctpublicdefendertraining.com/materials.htm.

cccxxv
Attorney Erin Schaffer, New Haven Legal Assistance Assoc. Inc., *Collateral Consequences of Arrest and/or Conviction on Education*, Public Defender Service Training (October, 2013) *materials available at* http://ctpublicdefendertraining.com/materials.htm.

cccxxvi
Attorney Sarah Eagan, Office of the Child Advocate, *Collateral Consequences of Arrest, Incarceration, and Conviction for Parental Rights*, Public Defender Services Training (October 7, 2013), *materials available at* http://ctpublicdefendertraining.com/materials.htm.

cccxxvii
Attorney Anthony Collins and Attorney Elisa Villa, *Collateral Consequences of Arrest, Incarceration and Conviction, Addressing Immigration Issues in Criminal Court Proceedings,* Public Defender Services Training (October, 2013), *materials available at* http://ctpublicdefendertraining.com/materials.htm.

cccxxviii
J. McGregor Smyth, Jr., "From Arrest to Reintegration,*" supra.*

cccxxix
Judges' Waiver C.G.S. §54-56g, 52 - 259b, P.A. 13-310, Program fees (C.G.S. §54-56e(b), §54-56e(d) Accelerated Pretrial Rehabilitation (AR) $35 application fee, $100 program fee. C.G.S §54-56g(a),(b),(c), Pretrial Alcohol Education Program (AEP), $100 application fee, $100 evaluation fee, $350 non-refundable program fee for 10 session program, $500 non-refundable fee for 15 session intervention program; person is also responsible for costs of any court-ordered substance abuse treatment program. Court may waive some portion or all of treatment program costs if person is indigent. Reinstatement fee of $175, $250 for 10/15 sessions. C.G.S. §54-56i Pretrial Drug Education Program (DEP) $100 application fee, $100 nonrefundable program fee, $350 ten-session program fee, $500 program fee for 15 sessions. Reinstatement fees $175, $250.

cccxxx
Data compiled by Ivan Kuzyk, State of Connecticut Office of Policy and Management, Criminal Justice Division. *See also,* Russ Immarigeon and Judith Greene, Diversion Works, supra.

cccxxxi
Court Support Services Division, Adult Bail/IAR (Intake, Assessment, Referral). http://jud.ct.gov/cssd/bail_faq.htm.

cccxxxii
Id.

cccxxxiii
Community Court sites in Hartford and Waterbury (GA4) *Guide to Special Sessions & Diversionary Programs in Connecticut,* Superior Court Criminal Division, Hartford.Commcourt@jud.ct.gov. *Available at* http://www.jud.ct.gov/Publications/CR137P.pdf.

cccxxxiv
Jim Tackett, State Project Director, Office of the Commissioner – DMHAS. Program sites : New London, Norwich, Danielson, Middletown, Connecticut. http://www.ct.gov/dmhas/cwp/view.asp?a=3833&q=450538.

cccxxxv
State of Connecticut, Department of Mental Health and Addiction Services (DMHAS), Forensic Services Division, Community Forensic Services (CFS), http://www.ct.gov/dmhas.

cccxxxvi
Kathryn Malizia, *"Assembly Line Justice," supra.*

cccxxxvii
Cynthia E. Jones " 'Give Us Free': Addressing Racial Disparities in Bail Determinations," 16 Legislation and Public Policy 919, 936 (2013). See also, Ian Ayres & Joel Waldfogel, "A Market Test for Race Discrimination in Bail Setting," 46 Stan. L. Rev. 987 (1994)(finding that in 1990s New Haven courts systematically over-charged black and male Hispanic defendants for bail), *available at* http://digitalcommons.law.yale.edu/fss_papers/1527/.

cccxxxviii
Douglas L. Colbert, "Thirty Five Years After Gideon: The Illusory Right To Counsel At Bail Proceedings," 1 U. Ill.L.Rev. 1998. See also *C.G.S, 51-296.* Designation of public defender for indigent defendant, codefendant.

cccxxxix
State of Connecticut, Division of Public Defender Services, *Annual Report 2013*, http://www.ct.gov/ocpd/lib/ocpd/publications/annual_report_of_the_chief_public_defender_2012-13.pdf.

cccxl
American Bar Association, *Standards for Criminal Justice 3rd ed., Pretrial release (2007), Std. 10-4.3* (commentary), at 94-95 (footnote omitted).

cccxli
Cynthia E. Jones, "'Give Us Free: Addressing Racial Disparities in Bail Determinations,'" 16 Legislation and Public Policy 919, 933 (2013).

cccxlii
Kathryn Malizia, "Assembly Line Justice," *supra.*

cccxliii
Justice Policy Institute "Bail Fail: Why the U.S. Should End the Practice of Using Money for Bail" (September 2012), *available at* http://www.justicepolicy.org/uploads/justicepolicy/documents/bailfail.pdf.

cccxliv
Id.

cccxlv
Kathryn Malizia, "Assembly Line Justice," *supra.*

cccxlvi
C.G.S. §54-82m. Rules re speedy trial to be adopted by judges of the Superior Court, effective July 1, 1985.

cccxlvii
Bruce Green, "Criminal Justice – What's Ahead? Roadblocks and New Directions," American Bar Association, Criminal Justice, 25 Crim.Just.1 (Winter 2011).

cccxlviii
Id.

cccxlix
Id.

cccl
Families in Crisis, Inc. Hartford, Ct. http://www.familiesincrisis.org.

cccli
Bruce Green, "Criminal Justice – What's Ahead? Roadblocks and New Directions," American Bar Association, Criminal Justice Section, 25 Crim. Just. 1 (Winter 2011).

ccclii
U.S. Department of Justice, "Smart on Crime, Reforming the Criminal Justice System for the 21st Century," (August 2013) *available at* http://www.justice.gov/ag/smart-on-crime.pdf.

cccliii
J. McGregor Smyth, Jr., "From Arrest to Reintegration," *supra.*

cccliv
Family and Offender Sentencing Alternative (FOSA), Community Parenting Alternative (CPA), Department of Correction, State of Washington, http://www.doc.wa.gov.. *See also* Arkansas, Voices for Children Left Behind, and Families in Crisis, Inc. (FIC) Hartford, CT. at www.familiesincrisis.org. *See*

also Raised Bill No. 361(Children's Committee) and Raised Bill No. 388 (Judiciary Committee), An Act Concerning Family Impact Statements, Connecticut General Assembly, 2014 Session. *See also* written testimony submitted by Attorney Susan O. Storey, Chief Public Defender, An Act Concerning Family Impact Statements.

ccclv
Center for Health and Justice at TASC, "No Entry, A National Survey of Criminal Justice Diversion Programs and Initiatives," (December 2013), *available at* http://www2.centerforhealthandjustice.org/content/pub/no-entry-national-survey-criminal-justice-diversion-programs-and-initiatives.

ccclvi
Steve Christian, "Children of Incarcerated Parents," National Conference of State Legislatures, March 2009, *available at* http://www.ncsl.org/documents/cyf/childrenofincarceratedparents.pdf. Okla.Stat.tit. 22, 22-20.

ccclvii
Associated Press, Beth Garbitelli, "Vermont Fights Drug Crimes with Treatment , Not Jail," March 16, 2014, *available at* http://www.publicopiniononline.com/state/ci_25355444/vt-fights-drug-crimes-treatment-not-jail.

ccclviii
Statement of Senator Patrick Leahy (D-VT) Chairman, Senate Judiciary Committee Hearing on "Community Solutions to Breaking the Cycle of Heroin and Opiod Addiction," Rutland, Vermont, March 17, 2014. Press release http://www.leahy.senate.gov/press/leahys-first-report-to-the-senate-on-rutland-field-hg-on-heroin-and-opioid-addiction_--

ccclix
Jennifer Laudano, U.S. Imprisonment Rate Continues to Drop Amid Falling Crime Rates, PEW Charitable Trusts, (March 14, 2014), *available at* http://www.pewstates.org/news-room/press-releases/us-imprisonment-rate-continues-to-drop-amid-falling-crime-rates-85899541906.

Chapter 11: Juvenile Justice Initiatives and In-School Programs

ccclx
President Obama has openly written and talked about using alcohol, marijuana, and cocaine during his teenage years. *See* Associated Press "Obama Gets Blunt With New Hampshire Students," The Boston Globe, November 21, 2007.
http://www.boston.com/news/education/k_12/articles/2007/11/21/obama_gets_blunt_with_nh_students/?camp=pm ; Jonathan Karl, "Obama and his Pot-Smoking 'Choom Gang,'" *ABC News*. May 25, 2012. http://abcnews.go.com/blogs/politics/2012/05/obama-and-his-pot-smoking-choom-gang/;
David Maraniss, "Though Obama Had To Leave To Find Himself, It Is Hawaii That Made His Rise Possible," The Washington Post, August 24, 2008; and David Maraniss, *Barack Obama: The Story* (Simon & Schuster, 2013).

ccclxi
Steven D. Levitt, "Understanding Why Crime Fell in the 1990s: Four Factors that Explain the Decline and Six that Do Not," 18 Journal of Economic Perspectives 163, 169 (2004).

ccclxii
The Juvenile Justice Act of 1995. "Juvenile Justice & Youth Development." Office of Policy and Management. State of Connecticut (July 28, 2012). http://www.ct.gov/opm/cwp/view.asp?Q=383628.

ccclxiii
Safford Unified School District v. Redding, 557 U.S. 364 (2009)(The Court held that the strip search violated the 4th Amendment.)

ccclxiv
Quinnipiac Legal Clinic, Yale Lowenstein International Rights Clinic, "Youth Matters – A Second Look For Connecticut's Children Serving Long Prison Sentences," (March 2013)
http://www.cga.ct.gov/2014/JUDdata/Tmy/2014HB-05221-R000303-Youth%20Matters%20Report%20by%20Quinnipiac%20Un.%20School%20of%20Law%20and%20Yale%20Law%20School%20Allard%20K.%20Lowenstein%20International%20Human%20Right%20Clinic-TMY.PDF

ccclxv
Connecticut Support Services Division presentation to the Criminal Justice Policy Advisory Committee, October 30, 2013. *Available at* http://www.ct-n.com/ctnplayer.asp?odID=9565

ccclxvi
Id.

ccclxvii
Dorinda Richetelli et al (Spectrum Associates), "A Second Reassessment of Disproportionate Minority Contact in Connecticut's Juvenile Justice System" (2009), *Available at*
http://www.ct.gov/opm/lib/opm/cjppd/cjjjyd/jjydpublications/final_report_dmc_study_may_2009.pdf

ccclxviii
Community Foundation for Greater New Haven (December 2011), 4-7.
http://www.cfgnh.org/tabid/547/Default.aspx

ccclxix
"Civil Rights Data Collection: Revealing New Truths About Our Nation's Schools," U.S. Department of Education Report (March 15, 2012). *Available at*
http://ocrdata.ed.gov/Downloads/CMOCRTheTransformedCRDCFINAL3-15-12Accessible-1.pdf

ccclxx
Community Foundation for Greater New Haven (December 2011), 4-7.
http://www.cfgnh.org/tabid/547/Default.aspx

ccclxxi
Community Foundation for Greater New Haven (December 2011), 4-7.
http://www.cfgnh.org/tabid/547/Default.aspx

ccclxxii
See Juvenile Justice Advisory Committee, Annual Reports, *available at*
http://www.ct.gov/opm/cwp/view.asp?a=2974&Q=383614&opmNav_GID=1797 See also, the "Right Response CT," Office of Policy and Management. State of Connecticut. *Available at*
http://ct.gov/opm/cwp/view.asp?a=2974&q=509812

ccclxxiii
Graham v. Florida, 130 S.Ct. 2011 (2010); Miller v. Alabama, 132 S.Ct. 2455 (2012).

ccclxxiv
Richard E. Redding et al., "Juvenile Transfer Laws: An Effective Deterrent to Delinquency?" OJJDP Juvenile Justice Bulletin, U.S. Department of Justice, June 2010. *Available at*
https://www.ncjrs.gov/pdffiles1/ojjdp/220595.pdf ("In sum, to date, six large-scale studies have been conducted on the specific deterrent effects of transfer [to adult court]. These studies used large sample sizes (between 494 and 5,476 participants), different methodologies (natural experiment across two jurisdictions, matched groups within the same jurisdictions, or statistical controls), multiple measures of recidivism, and were conducted in five jurisdictions (Florida, New Jersey, New York, Minnesota, Pennsylvania) having different types of transfer laws (automatic, prosecutorial, or judicial). The strong consistency in results across all these studies is all the more compelling given that they used different samples and methodologies, thereby providing a degree of convergent validity for the findings. All of the studies found higher recidivism rates among offenders who had been transferred to criminal court,

compared with those who were retained in the juvenile system. This held true even for offenders who only received a sentence of probation from the criminal court. Thus, the extant research provides sound evidence that transferring juvenile offenders to the criminal court does not engender community protection by reducing recidivism. On the contrary, transfer substantially increases recidivism.")

ccclxxv
The Sentencing Project, "The Lives of Juvenile Lifers: Findings from a National Survey" 2 (March 2012).

ccclxxvi
U.S. Department of Justice, "Report of the Attorney General's National Task Force on Children Exposed to Violence" (December 2012), *available at* http://www.justice.gov/defendingchildhood/cev-rpt-full.pdf; National Child Traumatic Stress Network Juvenile Justice Working Group, "Victimization and Juvenile Offending" (2004), *available at*
http://www.nctsnet.org/nctsn_assets/pdfs/edu_materials/victimization_juvenile_offending.pdf;
National Center for Mental Health and Juvenile Justice, "Trauma Among Youth in the Juvenile Justice System: Critical Issues and New Directions" (June 2007), *available at*
http://www.cwla.org/programs/juvenilejustice/ncmhjjtraumayouth.pdf; National Child Traumatic Stress Network Juvenile Justice Working Group, Trauma-Focused Interventions for the Juvenile Justice System (2004), *available at*
http://www.nctsn.org/sites/default/files/assets/pdfs/trauma_focused_interventions_youth_jjsys.pdf
("Due to exposure to traumatic events, many youth in the juvenile justice system have developed symptoms of traumatic stress. This fact sheet explores the role of pretreatment assessment, identifies important components of trauma-focused interventions, and discusses the treatment of co-occurring disorders as well as family- and group-based interventions that may be effective with youth involved with the juvenile justice system.").

ccclxxvii
Youth Matters, supra, at 9.

ccclxxviii
See, e.g., Rausch Foundation,
http://www.rauchfoundation.org/files/8413/5214/6585/NY_Breaking_the_Cycle.pdf
Washington State Institute for Public Policy,
http://www.wsipp.wa.gov/ReportFile/1374/Wsipp_Updated-Inventory-of-Evidence-Based-Research-Based-and-Promising-Practices_Inventory.pdf

Chapter 13: – Will Reform Threaten the Safety of Connecticut's Citizens?
ccclxxix
Michael Thompson, "Reflecting on Connecticut's Pioneering Justice Reinvestment Work," Council of State Governments Justice Center (January 14, 2014), Building Bridges Revisited Seminar at Central Connecticut State University.

ccclxxx
"Juvenile Justice Reform in Connecticut: How Collaboration and Commitment Have Improved Public Safety and Outcomes for Youths," Justice Policy Institute (Washington, D.C. 2013).
http://www.justicepolicy.org/uploads/justicepolicy/documents/jpi_juvenile_justice_reform_in_ct.pdf

ccclxxxi
Id., at 27-28.

ccclxxxii
Id., at 27.

ccclxxxiii
"Cheshire, Connecticut, Home Invasion Murders" *Wikipedia available at*
http://en.wikipedia.org/wiki/Cheshire,_Connecticut,_home_invasion_murders.

ccclxxxiv
Alison Leigh Cowan and Christine Stuart, "Suspect in Connecticut Killing Left Long Trail of Lawbreaking," New York Times, August 4, 2007.

ccclxxxv
Robert Gillis' February 2014 interview with Connecticut DOC's Director of Offender Classifications and Population Management, Karl Lewis.

Chapter 14: Dare to be Great, Connecticut – The Imperative to Act

ccclxxxvi
Juliane James and Suzanne Agha, "Justice Reinvestment in Action: The Delaware Model," Policy Brief, Vera Institute of Justice (April, 2013), at 1.
http://www.vera.org/sites/default/files/resources/downloads/justice-reinvestment-in-action-delaware-v4.pdf.pdf

ccclxxxvii
Id.

ccclxxxviii
Id. at 2

ccclxxxix
Id.

cccxc
Id. at 5-6

cccxci
Id. at 3

cccxcii
Id. at 3

cccxciii
Id. at 5

About *The Justice Imperative*:

Of all the countries in the world, the United States ranks 13th for quality of life and 25th for education. One area where the United States shines and beats every other country, including China, is incarceration. We represent about 5 percent of the world's population, yet we house around 25 percent of the world's prisoners. It is time for the United States to lead on a different path and *The Justice Imperative* is pointing the way.

— **Chandra Bozelko,** author of *Prison Diaries* and *Up the River Anthology*; ex-offender incarcerated at York Correctional Institution

* * *

There are 65 million American citizens labeled as "felons." And with it comes the reality and difficulty finding employment, housing and other liberties that are at the heart of the American dream. There should definitely be accountability and consequences for our actions but when does the restitution end? Our current system of justice brands a person for life with a scarlet "F." With the help of *The Justice Imperative* and other like-minded groups like Malta, hopefully that "F" can come to represent: FREEDOM, FORWARD thinking, FINANCIAL responsibility and ultimately FORGIVENESS.

— **Cindy Cloney,** ex-offender

Made in the USA
Middletown, DE
13 March 2015